Behind His COLLAR
FREEDOM FROM DIVINATION AND FAMILIAR SPIRITS IN THE CHURCH

Mable Ferguson Smith

Behind His Collar
© Copyright 2014 – Mable Ferguson Smith

All rights reserved. No part of this book may be reproduced, stored in a retrieval system, or transmitted in any form or by any means- electronic, mechanical, photocopying, recording, or otherwise, without prior written permission of the copyright owner, except by a reviewer who wishes to quote brief passages in connection with a review for inclusion in a magazine, newspaper, or broadcast.

Biblical scripture quotations are taken from King James, New International Version, The Message and Amplified Bibles, unless otherwise stated. All emphasis within scripture quotations is the author's own.

The names of the characters have been changed to protect the identity of the individuals.

Author's Photograph by: Christine Law

International Standard Book Number:
ISBN: 978-0-9894680-4-6

FOR SPEAKING ENGAGEMENTS
Email Mable Ferguson Smith: mef265@hotmail.com

Published by: Divine Works Publishing

Dedication

I dedicate this book to my husband Richard, my children Kendrick, Bertram, Alyssia, Rashad, and Amilia. To my family and friends who have cared for me, encouraged me, and even cried with me during this season of my life. Also, to all the women who experience demonic trials from the tormentor Satan and who seek enlightenment by the power of God.

Acknowledgments

I would like to acknowledge the spiritual leaders and mentors who assisted me in the process of writing and completing this book. To My Pastors Sheldon & Belinda John, Apostle John Chambers, and Apostle Kandy McBayne, may God continue to bless you and your ministerial works. To Wilmore, Lillian, Fabrette, Trevor, Sharon, Jeremy, Sherrylyn, Sidney, Dorcas, Zharmille, Nicole, Yanick, Willamay, Mavis, Jerome, Marianette, Shenique, Veronica, Desreen, Gary, and Cecilia; words simply cannot express my gratitude. May all power, and honor, and glory be to the Almighty God.

Table of Contents

Preface ....pg 11

Chapter 1   Innocence Twisted...pg 13

Chapter 2   Spiritual Growth ....pg 20

Chapter 3   A Different Thing ....pg 30

Chapter 4   The Courtship ....pg 38

Chapter 5   The Wedding ....pg 46

Chapter 6   The Marriage ....pg 51

Chapter 7   Heights of Manipulation......................................pg 61

Chapter 8   The Downward Spiral ....pg 75

Chapter 9   Darkness & Despair ....pg 83

Chapter 10 Restoration...pg 90

Final Words ....pg 101
   Healing Prayer for Defilement of Divination.........pg 106

Preface

It was a difficult process for me to write this book, due to the very nature of its topic, and having to reveal many of my own personal vulnerabilities and weaknesses. I also understand that this book may seem confrontational due to its story line and the titles and/or positions of the characters involved. My honest intent is not to defame the institute or character of the church, or any of its leaders who follow after the heart of God. This book is intended however, to expose Satan as he roams through our churches and our leaders seeking whom he may devour through the use of divinations and familiar spirits.

The issues mentioned herein are very real, and very much alive in the church today. I am fully aware that there may be opposition to this book by those who prefer to stay in darkness. It may seem as if this book is an attack on God's people, but only to those whom Satan has already deceived. For as Jesus the Christ has said [paraphrased], "If I cast out demons by the power of Beelzebub, yet I am writing or speaking against Satan, then his house will fall; For a house divided against itself cannot stand".

1
Innocence Twisted

It all began with an invitation to a Bible study by a close friend named Noelle. She boarded with my family and me, in our five bedroom home. I vividly recall her being as excited as she could possibly be, as she began sharing with me the details about a certain pastor who had been hosting home-based Bible studies, which she continually asked me to attend. "He's a seer", she exclaimed, "and he goes from home to home conducting Bible study sessions". She proceeded to explain that a seer was a prophet who could see and tell you things about your past, present, and future; this was something new to me. I had already accepted Jesus Christ as my Lord and Savior, and was attending a four thousand plus member Baptist church, was attending Bible studies, and was at one time a member of the choir. However, I was becoming complacent with the routine of going to church and to Bible study, at times feeling like only my body was there. I would sit in the sanctuary or sometimes in the side area of the church watching the big screen TV and hearing the sermon, yet I would still leave feeling like I was missing or searching for something more. No offense to the pastor, but it felt as though my soul was searching for a closer walk with God.

This irksome feeling was not uncommon to me. I had experienced this feeling before. I had been raised a Catholic from birth. My entire family was Catholic. As a matter of fact, my great-grand parents started a church in the local area where I grew up, right from within their home. They later donated the land to the Catholic Diocese to build a stand-alone church and my great grand-mother started her school for children, which later became the first catholic school in that area. All of their children, their grandchildren, and their great-grand children were Catholics. We alone would fill the church. I was required to go to every service they held on Sundays, and there would normally be three, sometimes even four services. There was the morning service, then Bible study at our church, and if the Anglican Church down the street was having Bible study for the kids, our grandmother would send us over there, and then there was the evening service back at our church. It would be hard to dodge church, because I lived with my grandmother and her house was directly in front of the Catholic Church. You could see everyone that was walking into the church and if you listened close enough, you could even hear the sermon along with the blaring songs. My uncles and the rest of my family would sing so loudly that you could hear them outside, even without them using a microphone.

Funny enough, I always liked going to church, it was natural, and it was ingrained in me. I was christened there. I had my first communion and was confirmed there, all at that same church. Growing up, I was taught the knowledge of who God was to me. God was important to me and I was important to God, so I always tried to do the right thing. I tried not to get into any trouble, not to stay out late, and I got home when I was supposed to. I also did well in school and attended church when I was supposed to. I clearly remember my first communion and the fact that we had to take classes to learn about the Holy Communion and the meaning of it. I remember learning that you had to ask for forgiveness before you actually took it. I even recall going into confession with the priest when I was about 8 years old and telling him that my sin was that my grandmother asked me to do something for her and I did not do it. He told me that God had forgiven me, and that I had to obey my grandmother and do what she asked me to do.

I would be in church so much that during church services I would recite along in the missal program for the church service as the priest read it. It got to the point that I had memorized the entire service. The only thing that would be different in the missal was the particular scripture from the Bible text for that day. I also recall the first person that I had heard of in our family that had left the Catholic Church. It was my cousin Sonya. She had begun attending a Church of God denomination, and I may be wrong, but at that time it seemed as if she had committed the ultimate sin against our family. I do not recall anyone ostracizing her, but I could sense that it was viewed as a form of dishonor. She however, was bold in her new faith and she was attending a church where they would jump up and down and dance in the spirit. I remember seeing her pass by our church, on her way to her new church, and always wondered why she had left.

Several years later, as a young adult in my early twenties, I attended a similar type of church service with my friend Mysha, and I really enjoyed it. It was interesting and it held my attention, because they were preaching directly from the Bible; flipping from scripture to scripture. It was very different from what I had learned in the Catholic Church. I was drawn to this kind of church service, and decided then that it was what I needed. One Sunday, as I was driving to the store I saw this church called Bethesda Baptist Church and the service had just ended. There was a large group of people exiting the church and I thought to myself that I would visit that church to see what it was like.

I asked my friend Mysha to attend with me the following Sunday. That same week, I called to find out what time the services were being held, and on Sunday Mysha and I visited the church. It was very good. The pastor was a prolific speaker. Once again, the service was preached directly from the Bible, we flipped from scripture to scripture, the choir was astonishing, and the message was extremely well delivered. The pastor had preached a sermon simple enough that anyone could understand it and then he announced an altar call. This was when they invited new comers or backsliders (people who were once in the church and left) to accept Jesus as their Savior or to become a member of the church. I continued attending the church for several more weeks, then I told my friend Dorothy about it. We continued attending together, until one day I whispered to Dorothy that I wanted to join the church as they were doing the altar call. I was too scared to go down by myself in front of the congregation. So I asked her if she wanted to join and she excitedly replied "yes!" We agreed to walk down together, and that's just what we did. We accepted Jesus Christ and joined the church. Right then, I understood why Sonya had left the Catholic Church. It was for a closer walk with God.

I was so excited about my new experience. We went through several weeks of new member orientation, where they taught us about the Bible and the church itself. We had to go through new member orientation in order to join any of the ministry groups at the church and I wanted to join the choir. Like Sonya, I also had an issue with leaving the Catholic Church. In my new found excitement about accepting Christ and joining another church, I went home to tell my mother the news and she didn't take it very well. She was concerned about how the rest of the family would handle it. It became a stressful issue for her; but she never told me not to do it. Eventually everything smoothed over. Apparently, it wasn't as big a deal as she thought it would be for the family. Thus, I finished my orientation and joined the choir.

In my new church I had never had, as my friend Noelle would call it, "a reading" and so I decided to take her up on it. We attended that Saturday and went together to Mrs. Shing's house for Bible study. She was a friend of Noelle's mom and was an avid follower of the seer. That night we met Pastor Phillips, the seer. He was a very good teacher and the Bible study was very informative. At the end of the study session Pastor Phillips prophesied to almost everyone in the room. At that time, I was in the process of selling my house and buying another and was concerned about whether I would be able to. I asked him about my house situation and as he held my hand to pray he told me that I was blessed of God and that I shouldn't worry about the house. That everything was going to work out for me with it and that I would get the new house. When we left the study that night I remember feeling cheerful and decided it was something that I would attend again.

Noelle and I continued attending the Bible study sessions, always sitting towards the back of the room, and not really speaking to anyone or forming any relationships other than a polite "hello" and "goodbye". Basically, we were attending to see what the seer had to tell us or if he would prophesy to us. Eventually, I began going by myself because Noelle was having more fun going to the clubs. After about a year and a half, Noelle decided that she was going to move back to Philadelphia, so I was all on my own.

I continued attending Bible study because I felt that I was learning so much there. It was always a small group of people, everyone got the opportunity to ask questions and get answers, and we gained insight that might not have been provided in a larger church setting. As I continued attending the study sessions, I felt that I was coming into a closer relationship with God. One particular night I recall, we were all in a prayer circle, and although I had seen people fall out in the Spirit before or speak in tongues, I remember thinking how it had never happened to me. All of a sudden, as one of the members of the group was praying, I suddenly felt very light. I felt as if I were on a cloud. I had been inwardly praying as I usually did because I was too shy to pray out loud when I felt myself begin to fall back.

> *Whenever we seek for information in the spirit realm beyond what God wants us to know, we are dealing with dangerous and deceptive spirits.*

It felt as if the Spirit of God had just lifted me off my feet and gently laid me on a cloud. I could feel my body as I lay there on the floor and I could hear the people around me but I could not respond. My body began to tremble and shiver uncontrollably as if I were cold, yet nothing was wrong with me. I laid there for over an hour almost seeming as if I was in a different dimension, giving praise to God. I now believe this was the entry point of divination in my life. Whenever we seek for information in the spirit realm pass what God wants us to know, we are dealing with dangerous and deceptive spirits.

As I began to stand, Sister Harriet helped me. Sister Harriet, was Pastor Phillips' assistant and right hand person. They would always come to the Bible studies together, sometimes in her car and at other times in his. She would read the scriptures and help to find bible verses for the pastor. They seemed to complement each other well in the ministry. He relied on her greatly and she was glad to be there for him, as if it was her only desire to please his every need. Pastor Phillips would talk with Sister Harriet a lot and part of that was because when he was not preaching, he seemed very shy.

During the service, Pastor Phillips was bold and appeared to have a wealth of knowledge about every subject. He had told so many people about situations that they were going through or had gone through. He would usually tell them how things were going to work out for them, whether it would be in their favor or not. He had a gift of prophecy and discernment that I had never seen before. He could look at you and tell you information about yourself that he could not possibly have known about on his own. He would have knowledge about your childhood, your current life, what he saw in the future for you, and even right down to the conversation you had in the car on your way there.

Although, when the sermon was over, he would revert into a shell, as if he were in a cocoon. He would not speak to anyone unless someone actually spoke to him or asked him a question. He seemed to be in a daze or maybe still on a high from being in the spirit as he preached, taught, and prophesied to the congregation.

The services usually went that way. Beginning with prayer and praise, continuing into preaching and teaching, then would flow into prophesying. The services would generally last two or more hours, but time usually felt as if it moved quickly.

2

Spiritual Growth

I felt that spiritually, I was growing by leaps and bounds. It was exactly what I was looking for, a closer relationship with the Lord. I began spending more time reading the Bible and I began feeling the spirit of God move upon me more and more. During that time the bible study sessions were being held only once a week with no services on Sunday, so I was still attending my regular church on Sundays. Pastor Phillips was right when he told me that I would get the new house and I was now living in it.

One night, I attended a Bible study that was being held in a home in Hiawassee, which was about 30 minutes from my home. The bible study went as usual with prayer, then teaching, then prophecy. As Pastor Phillips was prophesying to a member in the group he turned to me and said "I don't know what this means, but God said that He is going to fill your house." I smiled and said to him, "I know what it means." I had been living in my new home but I did not have much furniture in it. As my home was being built, I had put furniture on lay-away for my sons Kamrin's and Joshua's rooms and furniture for my sister Lyla's room, but I didn't have any furniture in my room except for a new mattress. My dining room furniture was out being repaired and stained, I had no living room furniture, the fifth bedroom was empty, and the sofa that I brought with me from the old house was in the family room. I knew exactly what it meant and it felt good to know that he was actually hearing from God and that God was actually concerned about me and my empty house.

He had not been to my house and he did not know about my furniture situation, so it must have been God... is what I was thinking.

As months went by, I decided to have a Bible study at my house and at the same time have it prayed for since I hadn't done that as yet. The bible study went well, and as usual, toward the end of the study the pastor began to prophesy. He told me that I was blessed of the Lord. As he walked through the house praying for it he told me that the person that sleeps in this room (my room) was a minister and there was going to be a lot of praying in this room. In the room next to mine, he said he saw a man in there and there was a lot of praying in that room also. At the time that room was empty. He told me that I was going to minister to women and that God was going to send another preacher to confirm his word to show me that it was not him speaking but that it was God who was saying this. He told my friend Cindy to watch me at work, that people were going to love me at work and they would hold me in high esteem because they would see the glory of God in me.

One day, as I was getting ready for church, Sister Harriet called to tell me that they obtained a building that they would be using for Sunday services and that they would be starting them the following week. I was so happy, because I really liked the Bible study sessions. There wasn't a large congregation, as a matter of fact there were only about ten people including two children and most of them didn't attend every service; but those who were there seemed to truly want to serve God. The services were held much like the Bible studies. There was a small congregation, very comfortable and open for question and answers after the service. As I started to attend the services there more than at my regular church, I began paying my tithes there. I would sometimes leave from my boyfriend Roger's house, which was over an hour away to attend church there on Sundays. Roger was not too pleased about that, because he said it was too far to drive just to go to church and I could find one closer, but I continued to insist that I liked the teaching there.

It seemed, at the time, that the more I attended Bible study and church, the more I was experiencing the spirit of God. There continued to be times that I would go there and just lay out on the floor slain in the spirit. Then one day as I lied in bed praying at home, all of a sudden the spirit of God came on me and I began to speak in tongues, but it was more of a continuous baby babbling, Ba ba ba ba, Da, da, da. I didn't hear any English translations or understand what I was saying but I could not stop saying it. After about 30 minutes of my baby talk tongues, it finally subsided. I just laid there for a minute and then I got up and called my friend Cindy and told her what had happened. I was so excited about it that I called Pastor Phillips and told him what had happened. I told him about my baby talk tongues and he explained that there are times when it starts like that. I didn't tell Roger about it, because he was not into the heavy religious scene and he had already told me that I should avoid trying to get too deeply involved in the church.

The following weekend Cindy and I went to Bible study. Towards the end of the Bible study the pastor prophesied to both of us. He told us that he saw us going on a cruise together and that we were not going to pay for it. We both looked at each other and smiled and thought that would be nice. A few months later Linda, my boss's secretary was looking in the travel section of the newspaper and she came across an ad for Royal Caribbean Cruise for the weekend, and it was on sale. So without hesitation she went online and booked it for her husband and herself to enjoy. She excitedly came over to the administrative office and told us about it. The price was so good, that Cindy and I thought about joining them. We searched online but couldn't find anything available for that same week. We had just closed out our financial month when Cindy and I went in to give Mr. Davis, our boss, the reports for the month. He was so happy with the work that he wanted to give us a small bonus. So I asked him, "Can it come in the form of a cruise?" He replied "How much?". I explained that it wasn't expensive only one hundred and forty six dollars for a round trip for each of us. He approved it, we went back to our office, found an available weekend and booked our free cruise.

When we went back to Bible study we shared with the pastor that his prophecy had come true and that we were going on a weekend cruise to the Bahamas for free.

It had been about two and a half years since I started attending the Bible study sessions regularly. One Saturday there was a guest preacher that sat in the back and just listened in. As the study started to end the preacher started to speak to me on his way out. He said some things to me that confirmed what Pastor Phillips had said some years back. He told me that God was doing a great work in me, that I was to stay right where I was with God and He would give me an even closer relationship with Him than I had right then. He said that people may not understand when I'm in the spirit but only I knew my relationship with God. He then said that I was going to minister to women, some men, but mostly women, because of some things that God had allowed me to go through. He told me that the best was yet to come. I didn't even know his name, I told him thank you, and he left the church.

The following week my friend Yenni and I were talking about God and the Bible during our lunch break at work. She had been asking me for weeks to pray with her at the office. Things were not too good there financially. The company was on the brink of closing down, business was so slow. It seemed like everything was closing in on us. From sales, to management, to banking, to payroll everything was a struggle. She felt that praying for the company might make a difference. Maybe we could help through prayer, but I was so afraid to pray out loud. I would always pray quietly to myself. There were people at the Bible study and church that could pray so fluently and it seemed like the right words would just flow out of them, but I was not like that. I never felt comfortable praying out loud; I always thought that the continuous flow of words did not happen for me as with other people. I just did not know what to say. I would run out of words and then end the prayer abruptly; but when I prayed to myself, I was fine. So, I kept finding excuses for why I couldn't pray with her for the company. I told her there was no space for a group prayer, and I would have to get up earlier to come to work to pray so that we could finish by 9:00 a.m. I never gave her a definite yes or no answer, but the thought of her asking me stuck with me every day. There was no good excuse in the world for not praying. I thought deep down that God was forcing me to come out of my shell, because I could not with good conscience deny her request for prayer. Finally I told her that I would come in the next morning at 8:30 a.m. to pray.

The next morning, I got up extra early, hurried to get dressed and it was raining like crazy to the point where I started not to go, but I had already promised Yenni that I would meet her there. The traffic was unusually bad due to the heavy rain, but I pushed through to make it there. I finally arrived to work at about 8:40 a.m. and Yenni was already there.

We went into the boss' office (Mr. Davis), since it was a bigger area, in order for us to pray more comfortably and we began to pray. My idea was to ask the Lord for forgiveness first, for everything that I had done that was not pleasing in His sight, then for God to cleanse me, make my heart pure and wash me so that I may appear before Him as white as snow and be presented before Him without spot, blemish, or wrinkle. I prayed that He would see Jesus in me, instead of me, and that I could come before Him to intercede for another. So we started to pray for the dealership, then for every department, and for the owner as head over the business. We prayed for wisdom for him, and for every manager, and for every employee that we would work to the best of our ability. Then I started to pray for Yenni and began thanking God for her obedience and persistence.

As I prayed for her, I heard God's voice for the first time; it sounded like my voice. I always expected to hear a male voice or a voice similar to what you would hear in the movies, with thunder rolling behind it. But God's voice was a reflection of my own voice and He said "you're going to preach". When I heard it I was shocked! I asked myself "Is God actually speaking to me.?" It couldn't be, but why would I tell myself that I was going to preach. I was terrified to pray out loud, how could I possibly preach? So I said to myself "No. I am not". Then I spoke back to Him in the spirit and said "How do I know that this is you?" And He said to me "the mere fact that you call me Father tells you this is Me." Then the voice spoke again, in my mind, and gave me two scriptures, Psalm 27 and Ezekiel 3:4. I was blown away and I said "Oh my God! God is actually speaking to me!" A thousand thoughts flooded my mind. Why was he talking to me? Why am I hearing Him? Why does he want me to preach? How am I going to preach? Then the scriptures came back to me and I could not wait to finish the prayer to see what they said. I knew this had to be God, because I didn't know too many verses in the Bible, at that time, except for scriptures like the 23rd Psalm.

Meanwhile, Yenni did not know any of this was happening to me, even though she was holding my hand praying with me. I continued praying with Yenni, but by this time the employees had started coming to work. Mr. Davis's secretary, Linda, had arrived at her office, and I guess she heard us in there, because she came in and joined the prayer. So I prayed with her, then Ilsa came in, and I prayed with her as well. As soon as the prayer ended, I told Yenni what I had heard and the scriptures that I heard when we were praying. We walked back to my office and she got her Bible and looked them up for me. First, Ezekiel 3:4 "And he said unto me, Son of man, go, get thee unto the house of Israel, and speak with my words unto them." And Psalms 27 "The Lord is my light and my salvation; whom shall I fear? The Lord is the strength of my life; of whom shall I be afraid..." I was in shock. I said "Oh my God, he was speaking to me!"

Right then another one of my other co-workers heard that we had been praying, and asked for me to pray with them, then another, and another. I did not stop praying that day until about 3:00 p.m.! I prayed for just about everyone in the dealership that day, including the owner. By the end of the prayer I was exhausted, fortunately my friend Cindy was there to help me through the rest of my day. I went home after work and could not believe everything that had happened that day. I called and told my friends Dorothy and Shantel about my experience at work. Shantel called me right back and prayed with me, she said that I needed to be restored or re-filled after praying as I had, so that I would be protected from any counter-attacks of the enemy. Oddly enough, she asked me if I was getting married. I replied, "No... Not that I know of." She said that God had told her to give me her wedding dress. I told her that Roger and I had not really discussed marriage, so we left it at that. The following weekend, Cindy and I went to Bible study. We told Pastor Phillips and the congregation everything that had happened. We were all excited as we told the story of how I prayed at the dealership for almost the whole day.

The time came for our cruise. Cindy and I were excited as we boarded. We had a wonderful time. She was so energetic; she wanted to do everything on the ship. Early Saturday morning, I woke up as the ship was docking into the port in the Bahamas. I turned to look out the window, and as I turned again to look at Cindy sleeping in her bed, I slipped into a trance. I had a vision of Cindy and Darren (her boyfriend) at her kitchen counter and they were getting married. The vision switched to show them at a hospital where Cindy was in labor having a baby, then it switched again to a vision of them leaving the hospital with Darren pushing Cindy in the wheelchair out the hospital doors. I said to myself, "Okay, so what did she have?" The view of them changed to a frontal view and I saw that she had twins, a boy and a girl. After this, I abruptly came out of the trance. At this point, I was not sure whether it was a dream or a vision, but I knew that I had not gone back to sleep so it could not have been a dream. It was the first vision that I had ever had.

> *False visions are lies that the enemy uses to set up his kingdom and to ultimately bring about destruction.*

Just then Cindy woke up and I told her about the vision. We were both curious about my experience but just left it at that. This vision never came to pass, Cindy never had twins. This was a false vision which is typical of the spirit of divination. False visions are lies that the enemy uses to set up his kingdom and to ultimately bring about destruction.

My sister Susan met us at the docks and we spent the day with her sight-seeing and touring the island. Later that evening we went for dinner at Jerome and Shantel's house (she's like a sister to me). As we were about to leave, Jerome asked for us to pray before we left. We all started to pray and of course, I started to tremble. I kept hearing my sister's name over and over and I figured God wanted to say something to her, but I didn't know what. Finally I said in my mind "What do you want me to say?" And He said "Say that, say her name." I said to myself "Oh, He's giving it to me piece by piece". Finally, I said "Susan", and He continued with the rest of what He wanted me to tell her. He wanted me to tell her to seek after Him, He desired a closer relationship with her.

That night, I learned something about God. He sometimes only gives you one part at a time. He doesn't always tell you the whole plan all at once. Be obedient to the first instructions He gives to you, and He will give you the rest. I also believe that because the Lord uses people prophetically to help others in their walk, the enemy attacks people with divination and familiar spirits. If he can gain a level of control in that area, he can hijack and/or taint the prophetic imagery and words being spoken. During this time that's exactly what was happening to me, I was growing in my walk and in my spiritual gifts, but the area in which I was ignorant was the area the enemy gained ground.

As months went by, I felt my relationship with God growing stronger. I spent more time reading my Bible, I continued attending Bible study at Pastor Phillips' church, and we had even started praying weekly at the dealership. Then one Sunday as the boys and I were leaving church, Minister Lowe came running out and asked me how old I was, I told him and he replied "Okay, thanks!" I thought it strange, but I knew where it was coming from. It wasn't him that wanted to know, but Pastor Phillips had sent him, which meant that he was checking up on me. A few weeks later, after church, Pastor Phillips gave me a teddy bear and said that it was a gesture of thanks from the ministry. I took it from him, but in the back of my mind I thought to myself that he had not consulted God on this, because God would have told him that I did not like teddy bears. I think they are a total waste of space. This gesture then told me that it was not a gift from the church, but a gift from him personally.

In all of this, I already knew that he liked me, however, I did not want his interest to interfere with me wanting to learn more about God, especially since it was at his church services that I was learning so much. So, I just put everything in the back of my mind. Later, another gift came in the form of pink bedroom slippers. This time, I concluded that he had consulted God. Pink was my favorite color and I had been thinking to get some bedroom slippers. My sister Susan visited church with me one day, after the service she said to me, "You know the pastor likes you?" But I denied it. She then said, "Don't you notice how attentive he is to you?" And I replied "I don't think he does, but if he does that's his business because the feeling is not mutual". He was not my type; he was older than me, very fair skinned, and quite old fashion in his attire, and wore a pat down Afro. Besides, I saw him in a more spiritual way. I had a reverence and respect for him as my pastor. There was no way that I ever saw anything happening between us. Roger was all I wanted.

A Different Thing

Roger and I had a history, although it was an on and off one. Ironically, I had also met Roger through my friend Noelle. She was his next door neighbor. She told me that she had a nice guy for me to meet. She said that he was single and it was only he and his daughter, because his girlfriend had left. She called him and talked with him and told him about me, and we began talking on the phone with each other. We spoke on the phone for about a month before we decided to finally meet each other. We met at a local Wendy's Fast Food Restaurant and basically just talked again about each other and about his car racing. Our first date was at the Olive Garden and our friendship grew from there. He would talk to me about his previous relationships and I would talk to him about mine. He would share his views on how he thought people were supposed to stay together especially when they had children. He told me that this was what his parents had done, and that was what he was accustomed to. He constantly talked about how people shouldn't just leave a relationship, because they felt that things weren't going as planned. He clearly had a strong sense of family and held strong convictions about not dividing the family unit. He was also disheartened and disillusioned about the failure of his family staying together. I admired that about him, I thought he was a great father and remember thinking that he would make a great husband.

However, he told me that he wanted to try and make things work between he and his daughter's mother. I couldn't argue with that, and I understood his position. I really liked Roger, but I don't think that I ever told him how I felt about him. I tried to call him a few times after that conversation, but he never returned any of my calls and I eventually gave up on him.

Then about a year later, out of the blue, he calls and tells me that he's looking for a girlfriend. I laughed and told him that I was seeing someone so it couldn't be me. Then he asked me if I could help him find someone. I found someone for him, but he didn't return her calls. He eventually revealed to me that he really wanted us to get back together. A few months later, my long distance relationship ended and Roger and I began talking again. We started to date once again and I was quite happy. We would meet up for a bite to eat or sometimes I would go to his car races.

One night, he told me that he wanted our relationship to get more serious. His long term plan was for us to consider spending more time together as a couple, possibly move in together, either in his house or mine then later get engaged and married. Most of his thoughts were fine with me, because I thought he was the total package for me.

> *God will stretch and challenge us out of our comfort zones, but tormenting is simply not His nature.*

Then one day I was sitting at my desk at work and I rested my head back on the chair and began to pray within myself, when all of a sudden a vision appeared to me. I saw myself in a Cinderella carriage all dressed up in Cinderella gown with tiara and all. I was getting married. I was all smiles in front of the castle at Disney World and I stretched my hand out to a gentleman, my husband to be. At first I could only see the arm of his suit and he was wearing a uniform. Then I saw the full uniform and he was dressed as a prince at a Cinderella's ball. I looked up at the face and it wasn't Roger, it was Pastor Phillips and he was all smiles also! I uttered in the vision, "What are you smiling about?" And at my desk I burst into tears. I sat there and I cried and cried. Cindy came into my office and asked what was wrong and I told her about the vision and she tried to comfort me. She called in Gart and Mr. Davis and they tried to console me. I didn't understand why I would have that vision. Why wasn't it Roger in the vision? Did that mean that God wanted me to marry my pastor? That was not who I wanted to marry. I left work and was still tormented by the vision. Looking back now, the fact in itself that it was tormenting me should have been an indicator as to its source. God will stretch and challenge us out of our comfort zones, but tormenting is simply not His nature.

By the time Saturday came around, I was still out of it. I wasn't my usual self, feeling dazed and downhearted. I questioned the vision for weeks. I had spoken with my friend and some coworkers trying to attain a clearer understanding about visions. Jerome and Shantel began to tell me about how they got together. Shantel said that God also revealed to her who her husband was to be. As she walked by him in church the Holy Spirit spoke to her and told her that was her husband. She was against it, because Jerome was not her type either. Jerome also revealed that Shantel was not his type. Shantel was always allergic to perfumes and scents; but on a trip out of town, Jerome was inspired by the Holy Spirit to buy a certain body splash for Shantel, who reluctantly accepted the gift. To this day, it's the only scented spray she isn't allergic to. They explained to me that they both had to get used to the idea, but their relationship developed and eventually they happily married. This added all the more to my already confused state.

Then one day, I attended a church service held by a preacher/prophet named Kara, whom I had grown up with in Hiawassee. I respected this person as someone who was close to God and clearly heard His voice. I told her that I had a vision that I was getting married, but that it wasn't who I wanted it to be. I told her that I was very confused about it. I asked her to pray about it for me and tell me what she heard from God. The following Monday, Yenni came to me and said as she was praying, God asked her why she was going against Him on this, doesn't she believe that He is in the midst of this. She said that she replied, "But Lord if You are in this, then why does Mable feel the way she does? She's crying all the time and she doesn't want this". She said that His answer was not to fight against Him on this.

A few days later I spoke back with Prophet Kara again. She told me that God had great things in store for me and a great work for me to do. She also said that she saw me getting married and then said "And the person looks like a preacher." I was crushed, those last words were not what I wanted to hear and I started crying again.

For the next few weeks, I was depressed. One day Sister Harriet called and said she and Pastor Phillips had noticed a change in me and he had told her to ask me what was wrong. At first, I questioned her about her feelings for Pastor Phillips, because anyone could see that besides the ministry, she was head over heels in love with him. She admitted that she had feelings for him for a long time, but he told her that he would never get married again and had no desire to be in a relationship. I told her about my vision and how I felt about it. She seemed to be threatened by it and I told her that I wanted to be with Roger. I then said to her that Pastor Phillips was changing and she replied "What do you mean?" I told her that, when I first started attending the church he was totally against marriage and being married, but more recently he had started saying if he were to be married again and speaking about relationships. She realized that I was right and told me to just sit still and not to say anything more. She said that she would speak with him, but we agreed not tell him about the vision. I never knew what she said to him and she never called me to say how she left things with him.

By this time, sister Harriet had noticeably slowed down in her attendance of the Bible studies and Pastor Phillips was basically running things himself. One day he called me sounding really nervous on the phone. He started to talk about the gifts that he had given me. I told him how I felt about them, about how I thought he had not consulted God on the teddy bear, but that the slippers were my favorite color. I also mentioned to him about Minister Lowe asking me my age. We also spoke about Sister Harriet. He said that he had asked her a few weeks ago to find out what was wrong with me, but that she never said anything. Then I told him about my vision, how I cried when I saw that it was him, and how I wanted it to be Roger in the vision. I told him that I needed him to talk with God about it and to ask God to change His mind. He replied that he would.

About a week later I had two other visions. The first was at the chapel at Disney World again in my Cinderella gown and Pastor Phillips was in his prince attire and we were getting married. I recall saying in my vision, if this is happening, show me the preacher that's performing the ceremony. I saw the face of a man that I had never seen before. He was average height, fair skin color and wavy curled hair. His hair line was set a bit back so that you saw more of his forehead and he had what I would call a cowlick hair line. His face was smooth and he was a handsome guy.

The second was a vision of the Cinderella castle at Disney World again, but switched to a reception with Pastor Phillips and I feeding each other a piece of the wedding cake. We were in our wedding attire with the cake on a stand in the middle of us and then I came out of the vision. I began to cry again, because I felt that God was forcing me to do this. I called Pastor Phillips on the phone all angry and crying and I said to him "I thought you were going to tell God to change His mind about the vision" and he said that he did. I said to him "Well, He's not listening, because I had another vision." I was on the phone crying to Pastor Phillips, telling him that I wanted to be with Roger and that I felt that God was forcing me to do this. I didn't want to leave Roger, but at the same time I was deathly afraid of disobeying God. So we talked on the phone as he tried to console me and stop me from crying. Still trying to get an understanding of the visions, I asked him about the meaning of the Disney theme in the vision. Pastor Phillips said that it was probably a familiar setting for me, something or some place that was pleasant for me and that may be God's way of giving information to me gently. Everyone in my family and my friends knew that I loved Disney World and would go there three to five times a year and I never get tired of it.

At that time I accepted his explanation, because it seemed reasonable to me. I have since learned that we have to be able to discern the source of the information that may come through prophecy, visions, or teaching of the word. I may have had the visions, but were they from God and was it of God? I had often heard about the different levels of heaven, but never quite understood what resided within each. I learned that the first heaven is earth and it's sky (Gen. 1;20-22, Deut. 11:11). The second heaven, is an unseen realm where evil spirits, divination, sorcery, and psychic abilities exist. This is where Satan is free to roam. Satan moves about through the first and second heaven and is referred to as the prince of this world (Gen 1:14, Ezek 28:13-18, Job 1:7, John 12:31). In the third heaven is where God's throne is and where Jesus is seated at His right hand. Angels have access into to all three heavens (2 cor 12:1-4, Eph 1:20, Deut 10:14, Rev 14:16, Heb 12:22). We must discern whether the information that we receive is coming from the second or third heaven. The Bible tells us to try the Spirit by the Spirit (1 John 4:1), and that we should determine false prophets by their fruits (Matt 7:16).

I still tried to pray to God for Him to change His mind, but I got nothing. I told my friend Dorothy the only thing I heard when I prayed again was that He would take care of Roger and that I wouldn't have to do anything. Roger was having a barbecue at his house and some of his family was there. As I sat on the couch and looked around, everyone was enjoying themselves and the food. I thought to myself how I wanted to be a part of this family. I sat there and began to cry. I tried to hide it but his mother noticed me. She began to talk to me and I told her how I was feeling with wanting to be a part of this family but that I felt that God was pulling me in another direction, but that I still had not spoken to Roger about it.

In December of that year, Roger and I attended the office Christmas party. He picked me up at my house looking incredibly handsome in his suit and we left for the party. We were having a nice time enjoying the company of the office staff members, the music, the dancing and the food, but inside I was still feeling depressed. Roger and I decided to dance a slow song. As we were dancing Roger said to me, "I feel like I'm fighting against God for you" and I replied to him "Then why don't you come on God's side?" And he replied "It's not time yet, I can't do that yet". That was our first time dancing a slow song together and it was our last.

A few weeks later, I told Roger everything about the visions and how I had cried and wanted to be with him but how I felt that God was forcing me in another direction. I shared how I felt afraid to disobey God, even to the point of something happening to him if I didn't leave him. I prayed with him and then he told me to do whatever I had to do and he would leave me alone. I knew that he was deeply hurt and I felt bad that I was the cause of his pain, but in my ignorance, I was fully convinced that God wanted me to be with Pastor Phillips.

4

The Courtship

Weeks went by, and Pastor Phillips and I began talking more and more on the phone. We, or maybe I, seemed to be rushing things right along. My thinking was that if God wanted this to happen, then it had to happen right away. I've since come to understand that just because you might think God tells you to do something, it doesn't necessarily mean that you have to do it immediately after he has spoken to you. Don't be so quick to move. Wait and get more instructions, before you decide to jump right in, because you may not have the full understanding. You may need more information before you begin your task, or it may be a task for some later time in the future, or it may not even be God.

Still, Pastor Phillips and I mostly talked about God, about what His purpose might be for us, about relationships, about the ministry and many other things. Then we began to go for lunch and dinners after church services as many church-goers do along with the other members. There was a Tony Romas near the church that we visited quite often. Then one day I was home alone and decided to call him and tell him I was coming by to visit him. When I got there he told me that God had told him days ago that I would come to see him. Once again we talked about God, about visions, and also about marriage. He said he had always wanted to get married on his birthday, which was February 14th. He had been married twice before, but I guess never on that day. In retrospect, the fact that he had two failed marriages, should have been another clue for me, but at church he had always blamed his ex-wives. Their names would come up often usually in a negative way, while he shed a better light on himself. He was always the innocent one. He would say his first wife Laura would always leave him for weeks and take the kids because she said that he was always studying the Word and he didn't have time for her. He shared that he had never wanted to get married, but she did, so he gave in. He also never wanted to marry his second wife Dina but it just happened. He said how Dina was a feisty person and always argued all the time. She had cheated on him, and eventually left, and took his little girl, whom he never saw again. Meanwhile, he was the good guy in the relationships. Both women divorced him, so he considered himself in good standing with God, never admitting what he did to them in their marriage.

During one of our conversations, I asked Pastor Phillips, "So do you plan for us to get married on this birthday coming up or next year's birthday?" He replied "Whenever, it doesn't matter". I told him that he would have to tell the congregation, because it wouldn't be right to make plans for a marriage and not say anything to them. He disagreed, but eventually decided to do it. About a week or two later at church, Pastor Phillips was preaching his sermon and towards the end he began to tell the congregation about my vision. He told them that he also had a vision where God told him to marry me. He revealed that he cried in response to the vision, because he never really wanted to get married again. I remember looking at him in shock, because he had never told me that he had a vision as well. In all the conversations we'd been having not once did he ever mention it to me. Later, I would wondered whether his vision had occurred before or after mine, or if he even really had one.

Yet still, everyone seemed happy for us so we all went to eat after church. Sister Harriet wasn't there, but I was certain that Pastor Phillips would tell her. We decided we were going to take a trip together and, of course, I decided on Disney. He had never been there and I told him I would be the perfect tour guide, seeing that I had been there at least 40 times. I planned the trip, he met me at my house and we drove there. When we arrived at the park, he seemed totally scared. He explained that he had never been around so many people in one place. He claimed that his "anointing" enabled him to see things about people and because there were so many people, he began to get light-headed. I had to lead him through the crowds. The gifts of the Holy Spirit, who is all knowing and caring had nothing to do with his getting light-headed. The anointing comes upon us in a greater measure, to strengthen and empower us, when we are actually doing the work of the Lord. Here was yet another indication that something was not quite right.

We visited about three of the parks, enjoyed the rides, and ate plenty of food. By the afternoon time, he had become a bit more relaxed, and we were able to enjoy ourselves. We arrived back at the hotel late that night. The next morning we got ready and decided to go for breakfast before driving back home. The trip was wonderful and I had made a new Disney fan out of him.

When we returned back home, I immediately began checking for places to have our wedding. Everywhere I checked was booked due to the fact that his birthday was on February 14th, and Valentine's Day sure was a popular day for weddings. I checked a few more places and was still having a hard time with the date. He and I discussed it and decided to have the wedding in Orlando and then we agreed to push the date out to July.

One day as we were sitting together on the couch he gave me a ring sized box. When I opened it, there were two engraved wedding bands, one for me and one for him. I asked him when he had purchased them and he said when he first knew we were getting married. He wanted me to wear it right then and I told him that it wasn't an engagement ring, it was a wedding band and that you are supposed to put it on at the wedding. He didn't care, he wanted me to start wearing it right then so I did. I then spoke to my family and he spoke to his, which was mostly his son and daughter. He mentioned it to his mom and sisters but they didn't seem to have a close relationship with him. Yet another clue, if you have issue with almost every member of your family to the point of no communication, something has to be wrong. When you especially have an issue between you and your parent (mother and/or father), anywhere there is unforgivingness and anger you're holding on to, that dysfunction will carry through to every relationship you have.

He seemed to have pent up anger inside of him towards his mother for something that had happened when he was younger. He had explained to me that all his life he had this anointing, and this gift of seeing. He was able to look at people and tell things that had happened to them and even things that they were about to do. He went on to tell me how it began to kick in even at the park, which was driving him crazy because there were so many people there and it wasn't something that he could just turn on or off, it just happened.

He spoke about his youth and how he was burdened with too much responsibility caring for his younger siblings, how he wasn't much of an outgoing person, how he hadn't experienced much in life outside of ministry, but in all that, I sensed there was something deeper that he held against his mother. He had also been distant with his daughter Tyaja, but had recently with Sister Harriet's help regained some level of communication with her. I spoke with her on the phone and briefly met her along with his mother, father, sister, and his nieces, when we went for a visit to his parent's house.

The very next day I got back to planning the wedding. I made a few calls to different hotels and got some prices. The morning wedding prices were more reasonable so I decided to have a morning wedding. I tried the Disney wedding pavilion but the price was way too high. The Regal Hotel gave me the best price for the food and ball room set up so I went with them. Next, I had to find a florist, a bakery and a preacher. I had told Pastor Phillips about the face of the preacher that I saw marrying us. He was close to two pastors, Pastor Chaney and Pastor Ellington.

There was a service that Pastor Phillips wanted the church to attend at Pastor Chaney's church, so I figured this would be the perfect time for me to see if it was his face I saw. A few weeks later some of the congregation went to Pastor Chaney's church service. When we first got there they were having praise and worship and the pastor hadn't yet joined the service. Toward the end of praise and worship Pastor Chaney came in and oh my God! It was the very same face I had seen in my vision. The pastor came in and started to speak. He was a prophet and could see things in people as well. During the service he called me out and prophesied to me. I don't remember much of what he said only that God was doing something with my blood and I went out in the spirit and was on the floor for the majority of the service.

After the service, I told Pastor Phillips that his was the face I had seen in my vision. He approached Pastor Chaney and told him that we were getting married and that we wanted him to perform the ceremony. Pastor Chaney agreed to do it, but required that we attend pre-marital classes with him for a few weeks. After we left the church, Pastor Phillips was angry that Pastor Chaney was requiring us to attend the classes. He said that Pastor Chaney had known him for years and shouldn't be requiring that of him. He also said that his anointing was greater than Pastor's Chaney, so he didn't want him to perform the ceremony anymore. This is why I also had to find a preacher. So I went online and started looking for a preacher, a baker, and a florist in or near the Orlando area.

Having to do all these things began to consume me for the next few weeks. I was trying to plan a wedding all by myself. Then Pastor Phillips called me one day and said he didn't want to do this anymore. He didn't want to get married. My initial response to him was "Well, did you talk to God about it? Is He letting us out of it?" For me, it was a perfect way out and I wouldn't be at fault with God for it. However, genuinely being afraid of going against God's plan, I had to ask him if he had consulted with the Lord. He hurriedly said that he had to go and he would call me back tomorrow. He ended up calling me right back, which I knew he would, because he had developed a habit of calling me twice. Each time he called me, as we ended the conversation and hung up the phone, he would call me right back to say something else. So when he called me right back, he explained that he was feeling sort of left out with me spending all my time planning the wedding. So I told him that I didn't really have any help in getting the stuff done but that I understood and would try to include him more and then he left it alone.

I had to continue getting things ready for the wedding and making sure that I didn't upset Pastor Phillips in the process. In hindsight, this was a glimpse of the subtle control and manipulation tactics of Pastor Phillips. While it was perfectly alright for him to have felt left out, his claim of cancelling the wedding plans without being honest speaks of a subtle form of control. He had never planned to cancel and should have just said that. Too many times we allow this subtlety to operate in our relationships without confronting it for what it is—lying, controlling, and manipulative behavior.

> *Whether a vision comes true or not is not the indicator of its validity, but rather its source determines its spritual legitimacy.*

I continued with more phone calls and planning the styles for the girls in the wedding party. I had picked out a beautiful lavender dress for the bridesmaids and had to decide between two others for the maids of honor. My maid of honor, Dorothy, didn't really care what I picked or what the dress looked like so it was left up to me, while my matron of honor, Shantel, came to town for hers. She also brought her wedding dress that she got married in for me, as she had been told to about a year ago, so that I could get it cleaned before the wedding. After finally deciding on Shantel's dress and having her fit it, we went home. As she and I were talking I started to walk towards Joshua's room with Shantel following when all of a sudden my head felt dizzy and I had to hold onto the dressing table. I began to pray and then another vision came to me. It was again a vision of the wedding, showing female after female of the girls in the wedding and also the maids of honor that were standing with me. The spirit of divination was at work once again. Whether a vision comes true or not, is not the indicator of its validity, rather it is the source of that vision which determines its spiritual legitimacy. Meaning that a spirit of divination may reveal things that are accurate, although its operations are ungodly.

Pastor Phillips and I had to make a trip to Orlando to meet with the hotel wedding planner, the baker, the florist, and the reverend. We went and met with the hotel planner and put down the deposits for the ceremony and the reception. We went to the baker and had to have a taste test of a few kinds of cakes and make our decision from the assortments that she had. We left and went to the florist and decided on the type and colors we wanted for the ceremony, reception, and the wedding party. He handled it very well and didn't get angry or bored.

My family and friends in the Bahamas wanted to have a wedding shower for me, so Pastor Phillips and I made the trip. It was his first time on a plane, and he was terrified especially about the size of the plane. It held about 20 people, including the pilot and co-pilot, but it didn't take long to get there. He enjoyed himself and met a lot of my family. The shower took place at my Aunt Margaret's house which was where we stayed. My uncle Joel took us for a drive before the shower as a diversion before the surprise, but I had already figured that out. He then dropped us off at my aunt's house. There was lots of food and many of my friends that I hadn't seen in a while. The party went off well and everyone enjoyed themselves.

5

The Wedding

Seven months later, it was time for the wedding. Pastor Phil (as I was now calling him), Kamrin, and I, were to leave that Thursday for Orlando and Joshua was coming up with his dad. I had to meet with the hotel coordinator on Friday morning and then the wedding would take place the following day. I had been working late trying to get everything done at work before I left that day. I told Pastor Phil that I would pick him up around 1:00 p.m. and that we'd leave for Orlando.

I saw that I was running late so I called to let him know. I wasn't able leave work until about 5:00 p.m. I arrived at Pastor Phil's home at around 6:00 p.m. I knocked on the door, but he never came out. I kept knocking and never heard anything. I called him on the phone and no answer. I then decided to call Minister Lowe to find out if he had heard from the pastor and he said that he hadn't. I told him that I was at his house to pick him up and go to Orlando but I wasn't getting an answer from him. So Minister Lowe called him on his phone and then he called me back. He told me that the pastor was home but not answering my calls or my knocks at the door. He said that the pastor was upset with me because I was late. Then Minister Lowe asked me to come by to pick him up so that he could talk with him.

I left to pick up Minister Lowe from his house and brought him over to the pastor's house to speak with him. He went in and spoke with the pastor and when he eventually came back out he said that the pastor wasn't coming out and wasn't going to take my calls. Pastor Phil told him to tell me that we could try this all over again tomorrow and if I showed up even one minute late again tomorrow, then we would try it again the next day. I was vexed. I understood that I was really late, but I thought he was over-reacting, not to mention that I had already scheduled a meeting for the following morning. So I told Minister Lowe to please tell Pastor Phil that I was leaving for Orlando as planned, and that he could figure out how he was getting there the best way he could, and I left. Psychological manipulation is a type of social influence that aims to change the perception or behavior of others through underhanded, deceptive, or even abusive tactics (6).

I picked up Kamrin and drove to Orlando. I wasn't sure if Pastor Phil would show up or not, but I figured that the money was already spent and I couldn't get it back, so if he didn't show up we would just be having a very big party with all my family and friends from out of town.

> *Psychological manipulation is a type of social influence that aims to change the perception or behavior of others through underhanded, deceptive, or even abusive tactics (6).*

The next morning, I met with the coordinator and confirmed that everything was in place. The whole time I wanted to tell her that I wasn't sure if there was going to be a wedding, but I never did. Shantel and her family came into town and I told her what had happened and she sympathized with me. Later that Friday afternoon I got a call from one of the church members who told me that the pastor was on his way up with Tonya and her family. I still needed to pick up some things so Shantel and I went to the mall.

As we got back, I met Pastor Phil, Tonya, her grandmother, Diane, and her two kids in the lobby of the hotel. I sat and talked with them as if nothing had happened and Shantel went into action. She had been secretly planning a little lingerie shower for me with the girls and was trying to get me upstairs, meanwhile Jerome was trying to put together a bachelor party for Pastor Phil, but he wasn't having it.

I eventually went upstairs and realized what was going on. My friends were all there. Dorothy and Mysha drove up together. Of course Dorothy's dress didn't fit, because she had refused to go in for her fitting. Some of the other girls were just trying on their dresses for the first time also. We were there all enjoying ourselves and reminiscing over old times with each other when Tonya came up and said that the pastor was looking for me. He eventually came upstairs to the room where we were. Jerome was trying to convince him to get together with the men, but he refused and also refused to leave the room with the bridal shower. Jerome tried to explain to him the tradition of the groom not seeing the bride the night before the wedding until the ceremony and he wasn't having that either.

Eventually the bridal shower ended and the girls left and went to their rooms. We talked about the traditions of marriage and whether either of us was nervous or not. He told me that while he was home God said to him "Didn't I tell you to marry Mable?" He said that God was adamant and angry about it, so he had to find his way up to Orlando. So he called Tonya and they squeezed him in.

We fell asleep and early the next morning Jerome and Minister Lowe came to pick him up to help him get ready for the wedding. All the girls came over to my room to get dressed and to help me get dressed. My sister Susan, and my friend helped me with my makeup and we all went down stairs. We were about forty minutes late. As we walked down the halls of the hotel all the girls began lining up in order of height with their partners. My brother-in-law, Susan's husband, never showed up so one of the groomsmen walked down with two girls. My uncle's suit had not been picked up, so he wore one of his own and he did look smashing. My dad and my uncle walked me down the aisle. I never thought I would be so nervous. I felt like my legs couldn't move. I literally had to lean on both of them.

Everyone looked so beautiful. Pastor Phil, Min. Lowe, Shantel, Jerome, and Dorothy were all standing next to the officiating minister. The ceremony went off after that without a hitch. After the ceremony, we all walked over to the reception hall and had breakfast. There was toasting, and dancing. We cut the cake and fed each other, but we didn't have the first dance, because of course Pastor Phil didn't want to dance.

I did a presentation in honor of my two aunts and my uncle. A friend of my mom followed with a toast in memory of her. None of Pastor Phil's relatives were there; he didn't want them to come. He was once again angry with all of them. The wedding went well and we had a good time after all. We went on a four day cruise for our honeymoon and stayed in Orlando for a week, along with some of my family members.

6

The Marriage

It was now time to head back home and back to work for the both of us. When we arrived at my house, Pastor Phil decided that he would go back to his apartment that night, because it was closer to his job. He decided that he would come to the house on weekends. I thought that it would be a short-lived arrangement. I figured that he would soon give up his apartment and move in with me, or that we would move somewhere else together. I thought it was crazy being newlyweds and not living together. This idea was something I had to get used to.

It ended up being months before we actually lived together, but in a weird way it was working for us. I kept asking him when he was going to move up, or if he wanted me to move down by him, but he would always ask if I was sure I wanted him to move in. He would always question his moving in, but we weren't getting into any arguments, so I would drop the issue. For the first few months of the marriage, we never argued and even we thought it was strange. Maybe that was because we weren't really getting to know each other, since we weren't living together.

We would get together every weekend; sometimes during a weekday, have Bible study on Saturday, church on Sunday, and then Pastor Phil would leave on Sunday night. He didn't want to give up his apartment, it was inexpensive, he had been there for years, and it was close to his job. So we dealt with it. It had been four months of marriage before Pastor Phil decided to move in. It was probably because his lease was about to expire and I told him it didn't make any sense to renew the lease again for another year and have both of us pay mortgage and rent. It would be cheaper to combine our overhead and pay one mortgage. He would have to drive the distance to work and use the money from the rent to cover his gas and whatever else. So he gave most of his furniture to Sister Harriet and moved in. All this time he had still kept in touch with her.

Not too long after Pastor Phil moved in, the owner of the building where we held the church services passed away. The building was left to the lady's daughter and she wanted to take it over so we had to find somewhere else to hold the services. I began looking in the same area where the church was but it was hard to find a place. Then I suggested that we start looking closer to home and he agreed. We found a place a few weeks later, I signed the lease in my name, and we got everything set up and moved in. At the same time Pastor Phil had been trying to finish filing paperwork for the 501c3 for nonprofit organizations of the church. He had hired a lady to help with the process some time ago, but she needed items from him and the two of them were not getting along. There were a number harsh arguments between the two of them, until finally he asked me to deal with her.

Ms. Suarez had also told him that she would rather not speak with him and she wanted to speak with the "nice lady" she had spoken with before. There was plenty of work still needed on the report. They needed the name of the church (which Pastor Phil already had), when it was formed, which days services were being held, the times of services, what the sermon topics were for a year and on and on. Luckily, as I was attending bible study and church services I would usually write notes down and the topic and the scriptures used so I had that information. I got everything typed up and turned it into Ms. Suarez. A few months later we got the 501c3 and that was a happy time for the church.

One day, Shantel and I were having a conversation when all of a sudden she asked me if I had been praying for the Bahamas or had some concern for the Bahamas. I told her no, that I wasn't but that I had planned to go there in a few weeks. She told me that it wasn't just a pleasure trip for me, that God had work for me to do there. I prayed about it and before I travelled God had me to fast. Time went by and it was time for my trip. God had told me that He would tell me what to do and who to pray for. I went to a church service and while there I saw people that he told me to pray for. Then my aunt had to go give communion and pray for the sick and shut in and I was led to go with her.

As we were leaving, the car wouldn't start. Some friends came to help us and it still wouldn't start. We didn't have any other form of transportation, so I started to pray within myself and said "Ok, God if You want me to do this, then You need to start the car." Right then I put the key in the ignition and turned it and the car started up. I thought to myself, "I guess He wants me to do this", so my aunt and I went and prayed for the sick and shut in. One lady that we saw as I held her hand and prayed for her started shouting the name of Jesus and said she felt His presence. I prayed with my aunt and it was now time for me to leave. There were two other people that I was led to pray for but didn't get to see them, so I left. I got back home and told Pastor Phil about my trip. He was not too enthused. He had been calling me while I was away and it was somewhat difficult to reach me at times, because of its remote location. So he was not a happy camper.

I later called Shantel and told her what had happened while I was visiting the Bahamas, about the people I had prayed for, and about those I didn't get to see. As we were talking the Spirit of prophecy was activated in her and she began prophesying to me. She told me that I didn't finish my work there and that God was sending me back. I was in shock! How was I going to tell Pastor Phil? He wasn't happy about my going there the first time. She just laughed and said "God will work it out."

About a week later, I was in the kitchen cooking and as I finished I fixed a plate of food for Pastor Phil and took it to him. As I went into the room, I saw that he was meditating and he then said to me "God said you have to go back to the Bahamas and I have to go with you." I was shocked on so many levels. One, that I was really doing a work for God. Two, that Shantel's word was true. Three, that Pastor Phil heard the same word that I needed to go back to the Bahamas; and four that God had smoothed everything out by telling Pastor Phil that he had to go with me. God really did work everything out. So we worked out our schedules and found the best time for us to go. God placed me on a fast again and we ended up getting a free round trip to the Bahamas on a yacht through a friend of mine.

We arrived on the island and I immediately began trying to find the people that God had told me about. Most were people that had been sick and God was having me to pray for them. We met one of the gentlemen at his house. I told him that I wanted to pray with him. I could tell that he was quite reluctant, but decided to let me pray with him any way. As we started to pray of course my hands began to tremble. I began to tell him everything that I had heard that God was going to do for him. At the end he hugged me and thanked me. I think God wanted to show this gentleman that He was here for him, even though he didn't think that He was. I was quite nervous, because of course I had to pray out loud but I got my task done. When we arrived back home, we shared with the church about our visit and everything that had happened while we were there and of course I told Shantel.

We resumed our church services the following week and they went on as usual. We would have some visitors pop in every now and then, but for the most part it was still just us ten members including the kids. Sister Harriet would occasionally show up. Pastor Phil would say that she was coming to learn about the lesson he was teaching then go and speak on it at some other church. It was a love-hate relationship for the two of them. He had put her out of the church before (around the same time that he had put Min. Lowe out the church) and then told the congregation that they talked and she apologized and it was okay for her to come back. Before we had gotten together, she had wanted him, yet they had shared a friendship for so many years that she had become his confidant. However, her departure from the church had put a riff between them. But things were beginning to change. Every now and then he would call her or she would call him and I would hear them talk as he worked on church matters in the room next door.

Ever since Pastor Phil moved into the house, he designated the room next to our bedroom as his place of solitude. He would go there to pray, read his Bible, or write out his sermons. He would be in that room for hours into the night, until he gradually began spending more time in that room than in our own bedroom. He would always say that he felt he was more spirit than man, and that he felt more comfortable being there reading or recording music for church. But while he was in that room, he began speaking with sister Harriet more and more, sometimes about different scriptures and sometimes on a personal level.

One Saturday night he talked on the phone with her until after one in the morning then came to bed. The very next morning at 6 a.m., as he lay in bed with me, he called her on the phone again inquiring of her if she would be attending church. He then proceeded to ask what she was wearing to church in a sexually suggestive manner, then he continued his conversation. I told to him to please go to the other room when he was talking to her. We went to church that morning, sister Harriet didn't show up, but he acted as if nothing had happened.

Pastor Phil also began using the computer more frequently in that room and he got a craze for it. For hours and hours he would be on the computer learning more and more about how to use it. I warned him that you can get addicted to the computer once you start to use it. Then one day, Pastor Phil was in the room on the computer, while Tyaja, his daughter, was visiting with us for the weekend. All of a sudden I heard her yell out "Ooooooooh I'm gonna tell Ma!". She ran into my room laughing and said "Guess what dad is looking at on the computer?" And I replied "what?" And she answered, "porn!" I figured "Oh, that's why he can't leave that room and that computer. He's been feeding himself with porn."

I guess I had thought that since he was a Christian, and I was one also, that things would just work out great for us. I thought since God had put us together, then things would be smooth for us, but once again in hindsight, God did tell the prophet Hosea to marry a prostitute, and I am sure they did not have an easy time of it. No matter who they are, or how they got together, two people in a marriage will always have to work at keeping it together. Pastor Phil would often say people like to say that Satan is doing this and that in a marriage, but there are only two people in this marriage, you and me.

> *Pornography is a sin, an abomination to the body. It is a perversion to the natural use of the body from what God has ordained it to do. It defiles the body and invites demonic and addictive spirits to come and reside inside of you.*

I began to see another side of Pastor Phil that I had only gotten glimpses of and more often than not that side began taking over. I felt that Pastor Phil was now being controlled by a different spirit. A seducing spirit was manifesting itself in him and it was probably introduced to him through pornography. His interest in porn may have even started long before he met me. I do recall him talking about how he would watch videos to show him how to please his first wife because he was not experienced, but after continuing to watch porn on the computer he took it to another level. He even bought a pair of male thongs and wore them to show me how they looked. I was in our bedroom lying across the bed and he was about to change his clothes. So, he took off the pants he had been wearing and walked across the room towards the bathroom without a word as if to see my reaction. As I looked up and glanced at him that's when I noticed what he was wearing. I shouted "Oh my goodness! What do you have on?" And he started to laugh. I was shocked and thought this must be a joke. I had never seen a male in thongs and didn't even know they made them for men. Obviously they do, but why would they? I didn't want to see my husband in a thong. It kind of distorts my image of a male. I didn't put the whole thing together until afterwards, that it was all a part of that seducing spirit taking over him.

More and more he started to change. The Bible tells us that a little leaven leavens the whole lump. Therefore purge out the old leaven that we may be a new unleavened lump. Pornography is a sin, an abomination to the body. It is a perversion to the natural use of the body from what God has ordained it to do. It defiles the body and invites or allows other demonic spirits to come in and reside in you. God ordained one man for one woman; his body belongs to her and her body belongs to him. We must remember that our bodies are the temple of the Lord. Demonic forces cannot reside there. They have to be cast out by the power of the Holy Spirit. Then we must flee from all such temptations, repent of our sins, and turn away from our ways that are displeasing to God. We must allow the Holy Spirit to sanctify us through prayer and fasting. We have to allow the Holy Spirit to convict us of our sins, become our conscience, and point us to the righteousness of God our Father.

There was a time when Tyaja called me from her house and told me that Sister Harriet called her dad and was making plans to meet him at her house. She did show up at Tyaja's house and Tyaja said that she made her dad go outside because she wasn't allowing Harriet in her house. When Pastor Phil returned home, he and I got into an argument over it. He left the house that night and came back real late. He just walked into our bedroom, lied on the floor, and began talking on the phone about the dinner they had just had together, and how she hadn't eaten all of her food. I just ignored him. The next day I called Sister Harriet and told her that if I ever heard that she was out on a date with my husband again, I would call her job and get the fax number to every office I could find at her job and fax in a letter telling everyone that she was seeing a married man. A few minutes after that Pastor Phil called me telling me to leave her alone. I told him he could not tell me what to do and that Sister Harriet could try me if she wanted to. I never saw or heard anything else about Sister Harriet again.

One day in church, Pastor Phil began to preach and teach as he often did, but this time I thought that he was way off course. He began to tell the church that God did not believe in step children and that God, neither the law held the man responsible for step children. I saw it as a taunt against me and my kids. He went on to preach about how God actually wanted the family with one mother and one father, no sex before marriage, get married, then have children. The way God intended. The order was God first, then man, then woman, then children. I believed that and I accepted that, but when he brought in the part of step children and the husband's role with the step children I thought he was off. Then the thought came to me, how could this be so, when Jesus himself was a step child to Joseph. Didn't God expect Joseph to play a part in the raising of this child, even if it was to protect His life from Herod? Didn't God speak to Joseph as well as Mary concerning the conception of and birth of Jesus?

After church I addressed Pastor Phil about his statement. He defended his statement by saying that Joseph wasn't in charge of Jesus, Mary was. I responded by saying that Mary had no job and was dependent on Joseph to take care of her especially since the order was God, husband, then wife. He just stayed quiet. We had now gone from never arguing with each other to always arguing with each other. Whenever there came a time when things were quieting down between us, he would start another argument. I told him one day that I didn't think he could go two weeks without having a complaint to cause an argument. He seemed to thrive on arguing, that got his heart ticking and made him feel alive. He wasn't used to living without arguing.

Many times he would wake me up in the middle of the night screaming out my name "Mable" to start fussing about something that upset him a month ago, something that I no longer even remembered. I told him, please if you have an issue with me let me know right then, because I'm not going to remember or know what you're talking about later. He would argue because he wanted me to lie in bed with him a certain way. If my right leg wasn't resting right between his crotch and my body slightly twisted toward his body and leaning on him then he would be enraged. He argued with me about his rechargeable batteries. He thought that I had moved them and he went into a outburst. The next morning he told me to tell Kamrin to have his batteries back in the room by the time he got home, and thank God Kamrin did.

There was a time that we went to Orlando. He went to bed happy and by the next morning he was upset with me because of a dream he had the night before. I said, "How does someone wake up angry?" I had gone from hating him being in that other room to wishing he would be in there all the time. I didn't know what to expect every night I went to bed. I considered it to be a good night if I was able get to sleep the entire night without him yelling out my name.

The demons he had inside of him tormented him daily and he then lashed out at me. Besides all of this, whatever happened with us during the week was shared in church on the weekends and would always paint me in a negative light. No matter what he would be preaching on, he would find a way to compare it to something negative about me. As I reflect, he began to slowly pick away at me until I didn't even recognize the real me anymore. I had begun to lose my own perception of me, of who I knew myself to be. When he wasn't talking bad about me, he was talking good about Tonya.

7

Heights of Manipulation

I had seen this pattern before. I remembered it from when I first began attending his church. He would use religiousness to cover his admiration or feelings for a person. Back then he would talk bad about his previous wives and talk good about me. He would say things like; I was learning so much, God's light was on me, God was advancing me so much in the spirit, I could do no wrong in God's eyes, I was learning by leaps and bounds about the Kingdom of God and I was highly favored. Well, he began to do the same thing with me and Tonya, only now I was the bad wife, the one that God did not favor. Tonya was now the one learning by leaps and bounds about the kingdom of God. Before he would have us take turns preaching sermons in the church but now it was mostly Tonya or sometimes his daughter Tyaja. He really liked Tonya and he basically waited on her every breath. One Sunday, we got to church and some of the others were there but Tonya was running late. He literally held up church until she got there as if God wasn't there until she got there. Even though he had said before that he wasn't waiting for anyone to start church on time.

On another Sunday, as we were getting ready to start the services, Pastor Phil looked at Tonya and said "Did you look in the mirror this morning?" And she being naïve started to wipe off her face and looked up smiling at him and asked if something was on her face. He said "No, nothing is on your face" and I guess he caught himself lusting after her and left it at that. The look that he had on his face was one of a ungodly desire and stared at her as if she was the most beautiful thing he had ever seen.

I sat there as I often had just watching everything play out before me. By this time, I had developed a mechanism where I would tune out when Pastor Phil started preaching his usual negative sermons centered around me. I had stopped taking notes in church because the preaching was mostly about degrading me in some way. I was there in body, but it felt like I was watching everything from behind a glass wall inside my body. I would pray about my marriage for God to help me to give me strength and for our marriage to get better. Every time we got into an argument and I prayed, I would always hear God telling me to forgive him, give in, be the bigger person, or it wasn't about me there was a bigger picture. I felt God was trying to teach both of us something and I always stayed and as I would say I just sucked it up. I honestly thought God wanted us in ministry together as husband and wife; or maybe He wanted to open my eyes and make me realize who He truly is for myself and give me as they say a message out of my mess.

A few Sundays later Tonya brought her boyfriend to church for Pastor Phil to meet him. They had been dating for a while, she had wanted to see what the pastor thought about him and what he saw in him. He mentioned to me that she was going to bring him but I'm sure that this didn't sit well with him. His little crush was interested in someone else. Well, he met Tonya's boyfriend but he didn't have much to say about him. He played the fatherly role as he later talked with her privately on the phone.

As time went by, Tonya announced that her boyfriend had her asked to marry him. I said to myself, "Pastor Phil will never let that happen." One day as Pastor Phil and I were lying in bed he said "Oooo". I asked him what was wrong and he replied that he was having a vision of Tonya and her boyfriend making love. I said to him "You better turn that vision off" and he said that he couldn't, but I knew he didn't want to either.

Eventually Tonya began to find faults in her boyfriend and she called the engagement off. Had I known back then what I know now, it would have been exposed to me that Pastor Phil was dealing with visions from the second heaven. His vision of Tonya and her boyfriend was not a Godly vision, but one of him peeking into Tonya's private life.

By this time, the dealership had closed down. Pastor Phil would laugh and boast about how he had told me he would pray to get rid of my job. He didn't like it when I went to work, because he felt that once I was at work, I ignored him by not calling him throughout the day. I would call him on my way to work and on the way home. He would call me in the middle of the day when he was on a break, but he wanted me to be the one to call him. He said that I wasn't paying enough attention to him while I was at work. There were times when I would have to work late hours to close out the month and he definitely did not like this. So he would always tell me that he was going to get rid of my job.

Well, not having a job also meant that my sons and I didn't have health insurance. I went on Pastor Phil's insurance at his job and I put the boys on the state's Healthy Kids insurance. I had some money saved, so I paid him back for the difference it cost him for my insurance fee to be deducted from his paycheck every month. I also had some money from a second home that I had bought as an investment for resale. When the time came to close on the investment house, because I was now married, Pastor Phil had to sign not on the note, but on the mortgage. He refused to sign. The realtor came to the house and he refused to come down the stairs. She said that I would probably lose my investment if I couldn't close, but not even that mattered to Pastor Phil. She went back to her office, but a few days later, she called me back and said she discovered that since it was an investment property I could close without his signature. I was so happy for that news, but I was also sad at the same time to see what a mean thing he was willing to do to me. However, that would not be the end of his selfishness.

I went to school and earned my real estate license. I began working at Hiawassee Realty and was required to be in training classes before I actually started selling real estate. One Saturday I woke up and told him that I had to go to the office for training. I got dressed and left. When I got there the owner said that the person scheduled for the training that day couldn't make it, so there would be no training session that day. Pastor Phil was surprised to see me back so quickly and I explained to him what happened. That Sunday in church he told the congregation that I was seeing someone. That I left the house in my sexy thong underwear and how I was dressed all nice to meet him at a hotel. He told them that I had come back home quickly. I could not believe it. I was angry and embarrassed, but I stayed quiet in church. How could he tell them that lie? He never said a word to me the day before. I never knew that was what he thought.

On the way home we argued the whole time with me trying to dissect his argument. Trying to show him how that couldn't have happened in the short time I was gone from the house. The realty office was about 10 minutes away from the house and I was only gone for about 30 minutes, including the ride to and from the office. I had another praying session to God for my strength, my marriage, or my release. Once again, He gave me strength, but not my release. So I sucked it up.

The time came for Pastor Phil to renew his health insurance, but he never told me. Every year he was supposed to choose whether to have me on the insurance or not. If he made no choice, then I would not be put back on the insurance. Well, I just happened to have a doctor visit when I learned that I didn't have any insurance. I called the benefits department at Pastor Phil's job and they told me that because he never submitted his paperwork, that I was not elected to be added to the policy this year. She explained that I would still have time to be added, but I would have to show proof of marriage and get it into their office by 4:00 p.m. that day. I called Pastor Phil and told him what had happened, he said that he didn't know anything about it or how it worked.

I had started a new job with a friend at his construction company as a permit clerk/runner and was being trained on the roadwork part of the job, going to different building departments and such. I went home trying to find a copy of the marriage license, but couldn't find it. I called Pastor Phil and told him that I needed a copy of the marriage license. He said that he had it locked up in his safe and that he had the key with him. That was another thing that I had noticed, he always wanted to have the marriage license in his possession, as if he had to guard it from me for some reason.

> *That was another thing I had noticed, he always wanted to have the marriage license in his possession as if he had to guard it from me for some reason.*

My co-worker offered to take me to Tyaja's house, which was where he spent his breaks, so that I could get the key. I called and told Pastor Phil that I was coming to get the key, he told me that I had better hurry or else I would have to drive even further south if he had to go back to work. I knew that it was not time for him to go back to work yet, and I could tell that he was just trying to make things more difficult for me. When I got there he came outside to meet me and saw my co-worker sitting at the driver's seat in the company vehicle. He gave me the key and asked me about my co-worker and I introduced them to one another. I told him that we were already on the road, so he had offered to bring me down to save time from going to the office to get my company car. He gave no response, but just looked at me. I gave him a kiss goodbye and told him that I had to hurry before I missed the deadline. My co-worker drove to my house and I ran inside to find the marriage license. I tried to open the lock and it wouldn't work. Would you believe that he had intentionally given me the wrong key? I called him back and he wouldn't answer the phone. Finally, Tyaja answered his phone and told me that her dad laughed after I left, he eventually told her that he purposely gave me the wrong key. He told her that I should not have come there with my co-worker. He said that I was trying to make him jealous, but he was the one who now had the last laugh.

I was distraught. Yet again, I couldn't believe that he could be so cruel. He even told Tyaja that he would often sit down and think of mean things to do to me. I just felt so alone in trying to make this marriage work. I couldn't understand our purpose. I often questioned why God wanted us together or was it even God? What did I do to deserve this treatment? What was the lesson I had to learn by being with him? And did I really need to know it? Did I really need to learn this about marriage or people in general? Maybe I was too naïve and sheltered from how hard life could actually be. Maybe God wanted to take off my blinders and my fairy tale view of how marriage would be. I didn't know what it was.

I later remembered that I had made a copy of the marriage license for my real estate license application. So I found that and took it to the office to fax it into the benefits department at Pastor Phil's job. I was so sorry that I needed to be on his insurance. If I didn't have blood pressure problems, then maybe I would have tried to do without it. As usual, I would pray for my marriage, pray for my strength, and then suck it up and as usual Pastor Phil would act as if nothing was wrong and we'd move on.

One day when things were peaceful between us, we sat in the garage of the house with the door up watching the cars go by and he said he was having a vision. I asked him what it was. He began to tell me about my next husband. He said, "Oh, your next husband is going to cheat on you and he's going to beat you" I replied, "What? What do you mean, my *next* husband?" He said "Yeah, you're going to get married again and he's going to cheat on you, with lots of women and he's going to beat you." So I said to him, "Are you telling me then that our marriage is not going to work, that we're going to get a divorce?" He looked at me and said, "I don't know, that's just what I see" and he left it at that.

We went inside and ate dinner. After dinner we decided to watch some television. He wanted to watch something about murder, something scary, or some crime scene as usual and I wanted to watch something happy, funny, or romantic. He turned to me and said, "You know, I hope that you are in a store one day and the store gets held up and you get held up at gun point. Then maybe you'll come out of your fairy tale land" I looked at him and said "Wow, I would not wish that on my worst enemy."

Ladies, if I may speak to you for a moment. I can understand that we all get angry sometimes and speak out of turn or lash out; but we have to make ourselves aware of what we are dealing with concerning our partners. We must posses self worth and not allow people to degrade us, call us anything outside of our character, and treat us like trash. We need to know the heart of the man and whether he means us any good. If Pastor Phil had truly loved me, he would not have wishes of someone holding me up at gun point. Love just does not act or speak like this. 1 Corinthians 13:4 tells us that love is kind, not envious, not puffed up, does not parade itself, suffers long, love does not behave rudely, does not seek its own, is not easily provoked, love thinks no evil, does not rejoice in iniquity, but rejoices in the truth. Love bears all things, believes all things, hopes all things, and endures all things. Love never fails. Please learn from my mistakes.

Pastor Phil tried to explain that I always wanted to watch something happy or some comedy or romance and that life was not like that. He said bad things happen all the time. People get murdered or lose their lives all the time. His opinion was that TV programs only project what is happening in the real world and I better had get used to it. I told him I was aware that bad things happened all the time, but just because I knew that didn't mean that I had to surround myself with it, nor did I have to choose to watch it on the television. I choose to surround myself with positive . He remained quiet after that.

The construction company that I worked for decided to go to an area that had just been hit with a hurricane. My boss asked me to go, because not only did I know how to take measurements for the projects, but he had also taught me to use the estimating software that generated quotes. A this time, I also did all the paperwork for the office as far as permits and registrations. I discussed it with Pastor Phil and he didn't give me any negative comments about not going, so I went. We went to Punta Gorda, along with the other electrical and drywall subcontractors. It was really crowded in Punta Gorda, and all the other surrounding cities. Many contractors had the same idea of finding work there. We started getting registered in all the nearby cities at the building departments, showing them our licenses and insurances, and filling out all the applications.

We started to ride through the towns and began finding homeowners and talking with them to see if they were interested in our company doing their repairs. By the end of the first day we had signed up with three clients to repair to their homes. We then decided to find somewhere to sleep, but all the hotels were full. As we were driving around, Tyaja called to tell me that her dad was upset that I left. He told her and Tonya that I was seeing my boss and that's why I went with him. Then she said that she had been telling him that she and her boyfriend were going to Orlando and Pastor Phil told her that he would go with them and take Tonya with him. I knew that he was trying to make me jealous. I told Tyaja that he never mentioned any concerns before I left. Why was he trying to start something now? He got on the phone yelling and screaming at me telling me that I was sleeping with Tony (my boss and friend). I was so embarrassed and Tony could hear the conversation. He told me that he was going to Orlando with Tyaja and he was going to take Tonya with him. I told him to do whatever he wanted to do and I hung up the phone.

Tony asked me what was going on and I told him parts of the situation as we continued to drive. We ended up riding a few miles back on the highway to find a hotel, but there was only one with one room available. My boss Tony got me that room and he left to find another hotel, because I didn't want any more problems with Pastor Phil. The next morning my boss came to pick me up, we stopped for breakfast and continued trying to find clients. We worked until almost dark and then decided to drive back home because the hotels were so crowded. When I got home Pastor Phil and I were not on speaking terms and I didn't go to bible study with him.

The next day when I got to work my boss came to talk to me and told me that my husband was not good for me. He said that he had heard some things that he preached about me from my cousin that was at the Bible study the night before; he told me that his wife Kara was going to speak to me. When I spoke to Kara, who was also the prophet from before, she told me everything Pastor Phil had said in church. He told the congregation that I was seeing my boss and that I had gone away with him. He told them about my underwear ordeal again. He told them that I never bought any groceries for the house except for when Joshua would come home. Again, I didn't understand why he said that. I bought groceries on Fridays which was when I got paid, and it happened to be Friday when Joshua would come over from his dad's house. He lived with his dad during the week for school, then came over with me on the weekends. Pastor Phil knew that, why he would say that was beyond my comprehension, especially knowing that he never bought any groceries for the house at all or paid for anything else for the house for that matter. He also told them about my menstrual cycle and when I liked to have sex. He told them I wanted to rush the wedding along, because I didn't want to have sex before we got married and much more. Once again, I couldn't believe what I was hearing. The tears began to roll down my face and she hugged me and started to pray with me and for me. Pastor Phil and I didn't speak to each other for several weeks after that.

It seemed as if one thing was happening right after the other. As one situation would calm down in my life, another would rise up. I was in the office one day talking with Conrad who was the bookkeeper for the office. He also had his real estate license and he began sharing information with me concerning real estate sales, commissions, and researching houses on MLS, which is a Multiple Listing System that lists all houses for sale by realtor companies, on the computer. He was teaching me a lot on the MLS, and I was grateful to learn.

A few days later, Tyaja and Tonya came to visit with Pastor Phil at the house. I happened to be talking to Tonya one day about school and classes and we got into a discussion on real estate. I mentioned to her that I preferred being at the office instead of being on the road getting measurements. Not only was I learning the office work, but I was also learning a lot from Conrad about real estate and the MLS. I told her that he had been working in real estate for a while and he had a lot of credentials and many certificates for different areas of real estate.

The next day Pastor Phil was searching my computer and looking through my e-mails and the contacts and Tyaja and Tonya came by again but this time I was at work. I was trying to get into my e-mails and it kept telling me that someone else was using my account. I thought it was strange so I went in and changed the password to my e-mail. I tried to get into my e-mail again and it told me again that some was in my e-mail account. It seemed as soon as I changed the password someone would change it again. I remembered that I had given Pastor Phil the codes to my computer so I called him to see if it was him. When I called him he started accusing me of seeing different people in my contacts list. He started asking me about different names on the list and I was explaining who they were. He then asked me about a Dean on my list and I couldn't remember who it was. He called off their e-mail address and their nickname and I realized it was one of my best friends in the Bahamas. I told him who it was, but he wouldn't believe me. He began to ask me a bunch of questions about him and I answered them all. Then Ms. Tonya chimed in and told him that I was talking to her about some guy that I liked at my office and how I said he had so many credentials and how I said I really liked being at the office.

I went ballistic! I couldn't believe she had turned the whole story around. Then he put her on the phone, and she and I began arguing back and forth. I couldn't believe that she was also accusing me of seeing someone, while she was in my own house. It was like she hadn't understood anything I shared with her about the person teaching me real estate and the MLS. She proceeded to tell me that Pastor Phil complained about him having to pay for my insurance and how he didn't have the money to cover that expense. I angrily blurted "First of all, its none of your business and secondly, I pay him back every month, so he isn't paying anything for me!"

I felt as if there was a whirlwind going on in my head. I hung up the phone and called Pastor Phil right back and told him to remove her from my house immediately. How dare she accuse me wrongfully and then sit up in my house. When I got home from work Tyaja and Tonya were still there sitting outside. She told Pastor Phil that she thought that was what I had told her still sticking to her story and he believed her. However, if I were cheating, she was not one of the persons I would have confided in. It made no sense. She wasn't a close friend of mine. As a matter of fact she was a close friend of his so why would I confide in her?

Tyaja came to talk to me and I told her that she was welcome but I didn't want Tonya inside my house anymore and Pastor Phil had better understand that. Tonya knew quite well what she was doing. He didn't argue with me and they left. There was now a riff between Tonya and me and we didn't speak to each other for a while. After Pastor Phil took Tonya's side in the argument, there was greater division between he and myself, while the two of them spoke more frequently and spent quite a bit of time on the phone.

Then one night, at the end of Bible study, Tonya walked over to Pastor Phil for some clarification on something he had said in Bible study and they talked for a while before we left. We got home and changed and went to bed. Around 1:00 am in the morning his phone rang. Before answering it he grumbled, "Who's calling me now?" He then looked at the phone and answered it. I could hear that it was Tonya. I guess that she asked him once again for more clarification on the same topic at Bible study, because he began explaining the same thing again. I was furious, why would she think that it was okay to call a married pastor at this hour to discuss something he just spoke to her about before we left Bible study? He got up from the bed and went into the other room to finish his conversation.

The following Saturday at Bible study, Pastor Phil taught on how Jesus was about ministry and teaching. He said that he also was about ministry and teaching. That it didn't matter what time of the day or night it was, he was going to teach his congregation. Then he went into the incident during Bible study and proceeded to tell the congregation about the 1:00 a.m. phone call. He had the congregation to give their opinion on how I reacted to the phone call at that hour. One person said that it shouldn't matter what time you call. Another went into a story that happened to him where his friend had called and left him a message for him to return the call, but he didn't until the next morning. The next morning he found out that the person had died that night and how sorry he felt for not returning the call. After everyone gave their opinion, I stood up and said that I understood if a person had an emergency, that time did not matter. I understood that Pastor Phil would answer the phone at whatever time, because he wasn't sure if the person on the other end had an emergency, but was also aware that the person making the call at 1:00 am knew beforehand whether it was an emergency or not. He or she should know whether that phone call could wait until a more appropriate time. I didn't blame Pastor Phil for answering the call, because he didn't know if Tonya had an emergency, but I did blame Tonya for making the call at that hour because she knew that it could wait. I told them that Tonya displayed no respect for me or for our marriage because Pastor Phil hadn't either. Therefore, she felt it was alright to call at 1:00 a.m. and he hadn't corrected her. No one said a word.

8

The Downward Spiral

A few days later our mutual friend Darlene called me all upset. She asked if I was by myself and I told her that I was. She proceeded to tell me how Pastor Phil had called her to talk about me. He told her how much he hated me and that the reason why he spent all his time in the other room was because he couldn't stand to look at my face. She said that he went on and on saying all kinds of negative stuff about me and that she felt so sorry for me. For a moment, she expressed some concern about him finding out she shared the conversation with me, but then she figured that she had already moved away and left the church, so it didn't really matter. Besides, she said that she had to tell me what was going on. She said that he also shared with her that he had mentioned these very same things to my brother who was living with us at the time. Once again, I was infuriated and I confronted him. We argued about it and then I left and went to the downstairs bedroom to sleep. I slept there with the room door locked until I heard him leave for work early the next morning.

The following night, as I started to fall asleep, he came downstairs to talk to me. He began telling me that I needed to come back to our bedroom and sleep in our bed. I thought about it and decided to go back to my room, after all it was my room and why should I displace myself when he could just as easily go to the other room. So I got up and went upstairs to sleep. No sooner than I got settled in the room, the conversation came up again about what he had said and we started arguing again. I asked him why he would want to sleep next to someone that he hated and we started arguing again. Eventually I just stopped arguing with him and everything got quiet.

All of a sudden, as I started to fall asleep, Pastor Phil shouted out my name. It stunned me, but I didn't answer. He shouted my name again, but I still did not answer. He then grabbed hold of my hair, which luckily was a wig I was wearing and yanked it off my head and started tearing it to pieces. I still didn't say anything to him I just lied there with my back turned to him. Suddenly, he kicked me out of the bed with his feet. I fell to the floor and I began to pick up the phone and starting dialing, he yanked the phone from me and slammed it against the wall and the phone fell apart. I got up off the floor, stayed quiet, left the room and went back downstairs and prayed and cried and cried and prayed but still didn't hear that I could leave. I felt so all alone in this marriage. I felt like I was being punished for something, but I didn't know what. God was not releasing me. I was so tired of my situation and felt that all hope was gone. I just did not have any more strength in me to fight this battle.

The next morning, after Pastor Phil had left for work, I went back into the bedroom. I found the wig hidden under the bed. He had cut out the top center of the wig and it was just one big hole. I looked at it and thought that he was a demented person. I spoke to my brother Sammy about what had happened and told him what I had heard and begged him not to say anything to Pastor Phil. Sammy had spent some time in jail recently and I didn't want him getting into any trouble.

A few Saturdays later, we were in Bible study and Pastor Phil was teaching from John chapter 15 on the true vine and the branches. Jesus being the true vine and we are all branches. Then he went into further explanation about a tree, its roots, and the branches. He then began to make reference about relationships and how you should find out about the person before you marry them; check out his/her family tree, roots, and branches. All of a sudden he turned it into a sermon about me. He said that he met my family and that I came from a good family. He said that my family had good roots but that I was a bad branch. He continued speaking to the congregation badly about me as I sat there in a daze. Then he turned to me and said "God said to tell you to stop coming to him about your husband." I sat there and I thought "WOW!" That was my final moment of despair. At that moment, I felt that even God had deserted me. That I was definitely in this alone with no one, not even God to help me get through this. Pastor Phil had painted a really bad picture of me and I believed it. I had lost all resemblance of my true self. I accepted Pastor Phil's word as truth, I stopped praying, and I gave up on God.

> Pastor Phil had painted a really bad picture of me and I believed it. I had lost all resemblance of myself. I accepted Pastor Phil's word as truth, I stopped praying, and I gave up on God.

I removed myself from God, thinking that He didn't want to deal with me anymore. I realize now that this was when the enemy had come in to take over. I would lie in bed with Pastor Phil next to me thinking of ways to end my life, just be done with this mess. But, every time I would think of killing myself my thoughts would go to Kamrin and Joshua and how I didn't want to not be there for them. They were too young for me to leave them.

A few weeks later, my sister Susan was in town from the Bahamas and I didn't go to Bible study that Saturday. Tyaja called me, sounding all frantic on the phone. She told me all the nasty details that Pastor Phil had said about me during Bible study the night before. He brought up everything again. All about my underwear, about having sex with me, about my tampons, about me having an affair and everything else I guess he could think of. I was furious! I felt that it was an assassination of my character and I had enough of him and his lies. He had taken me to the highest point of infuriation!

As I think back over my life, the only physical fight that I can remember having was in the fifth grade and it was because of lies. I was never a fighter, I was always laid back and easy going except for that one time when Winter Raymonds told a lie about me and blamed me for starting gossip about our classmate, when she knew she was the one who had started it. I was so angry that I just lost my cool. I fussed her out and told her not to handle my name with any of her lies. She tried to deny it and I threw the first punch. It was an unction that had risen up in me then, and a similar righteous indignation was rising up on the inside me at that moment. I knew that I had to defend myself.

My sister and her kids were at the house and Pastor Phil had already left for church. So I made plans to go to the church and tell the congregation everything that he had done to me and also the things that he had said about them. My sister decided that she would come along with her kids and mine. I didn't think it would turn out the way that it did.

We got to the service and we all sat at the back of the church. Pastor Phil was preaching and I was seething. As he was about to end the service, I raised my hand and he me asked if I had something to say. I asked him if I could address the church and he answered "Yes." I got up and told the church that I had heard all about Pastor Phil's sermon about me and that I wanted to clear some things. I explained about my underwear issue and how he assumed that I was having an affair because I wore sexy underwear to go to my training at the real estate office. The time that I had left the house and had come back was all of thirty minutes at most. I explained that when I arrived there, the training was cancelled because the trainer didn't show up. The reason for that type of underwear was because I had not done the laundry and that was what was left in the drawer. I told them how he had accused me for months of liking Minister Lowe. He would have Lowe talk to me for him in the beginning then he told Minister Lowe that I liked him. Minister Lowe told Pastor Phil that he could tell when someone liked him and that I did not like him. Then I told them about what he did to me concerning the health insurance. I told them about him and Sister Harriet talking back and forth until all hours of the morning. How they went out for dinner one night and how he came back and continued talking with her on the phone as he lay next to me. I told them about how he told me that in the spirit he had seen Tonya and her boyfriend having sex, and how I told him to turn it off and he said that he couldn't but he was really lusting after Tonya. I told them that he had expressed to my family that he hated me. I told them that he had said one of the members named Shirley did not have the Holy Ghost in her and how he didn't think that she was saved. How he was tired of Marvin and his wife calling him for marriage counseling and he was tired of their arguments. I also told them how he had said that all the church members were just a bunch of dumb church folks.

Then Pastor Phil came up and started to speak. He admitted to the things that he said about Shirley and Marvin and his wife and then started to talk about me again and admitted that he did say that he hated me. Then my sister Susan stood up and said if you hate her so much then why are you still there, you need to leave. Then Pastor Phil said that he was still there because he was saving up his money to be able to move. Then Susan told him not to stay there and use her sister to wait and save money. "Go now," she proclaimed firmly, "be a man, stand on your own two feet, and go now". She further urged him to go and live with his daughter. Right then Tonya attempted to verbally attack me and said, "Well, Mable you've said something about everyone but what about you? You didn't say anything about yourself." I responded, "Tonya, what else do you need to know about me that Pastor Phil hasn't already told the entire church?". She looked blankly at me and remained quiet. As if all that were not enough, Pastor Phil began talking about me again and my son Kamrin became enraged. Tonya started with me once again, when suddenly Kamrin leaped from the back of the church lunging toward Tonya while tossing all the chairs out of his way. At that point, everyone stood up trying to hold him down. Then Tyaja, Pastor Phil's daughter ran over as if to fight and protect Tonya. Then my sister

Susan told Pastor Phil that by the time he got home his stuff would be outside. Marvin and I continued to hold Kamrin down to try to calm the situation. I instructed my family to go out to the car, as Marvin tried to hold Kamrin so that I could take him out of there. No one actually ever did fight but the situation did get ugly. I had to ask for forgiveness for that whole incident. When we got home Susan and I packed up all of Pastor Phil's stuff and put them at the front door. Later that day, he and Tyaja came by and picked them up and they left. I called my friend and boss Tony to come by and change the locks on the door.

I had so many emotions going on inside of me all at the same time. I was relieved, happy, sad, confused, and terrified all wrapped into one. I was relieved that my turmoil might be finished. I was definitely happy that he was out of the house. I was sad that my marriage was not working out. I was confused as to why we were where we were right then and terrified that I was disappointing God. I still didn't know for sure that God had released me from this marriage.

At this point, I couldn't go back to Pastor Phil's church. I started attending Kara's Bible studies and visiting different churches. I did this for about two months trying to make sense of everything. At one of Kara's Bible studies, during prayer, I heard a voice say to me "This is where you belong." I questioned it, because I took it to mean that I should not be at Pastor Phil's church. Eventually Tyaja started calling me and we would talk back and forth. Pastor Phil had moved in with her. He and I also began to talk again over the phone and tried to go over everything that had happened. He invited me to one of the Bible study services and I did go, believing I had not been released from my marriage. Being there felt awkward, because it was my first time back since the incident at the church, but everyone was kind to me and they welcomed me back.

From that point forward, I continued visiting Pastor Phil's church and still continued to attend Kara's Bible studies. One day at Pastor Phil's church service he was "in the spirit" and he looked at me and said "You heard something at Kara's Bible study that confused you, but God said to tell you not to take it out of context." I figured that meant that I was to attend both places, which was what I was doing. He also started to tell the church, while he was in a trance about all the things that he had done wrong and that it was not my fault. I just sat there at looked at him with surprise as did everyone else. One of the ladies of the church just looked at me and smiled. As Pastor Phil talked, I just felt vindicated, I felt that God was finally letting them know the truth. I also felt that God was telling me to forgive Tonya and I did. At the end of the service Pastor Phil told the church that God had revealed to him that he would not marry again. Tyaja jumped up and said in a joking manner "Of course not fool, you're already married to Ma," which is what she called me. I looked at him strangely. What did that mean? Why would he say that? Would we be getting a divorce? Did he know something that I didn't? After that, we all left the church and Pastor Phil went to my house with me for dinner.

I guess you could say, Pastor Phil and I began dating each other again. He was still living with his daughter Tyaja, and I lived in my house. Every now and then, he would come over for dinner, or we would meet somewhere, but he never moved back in.

One day I went to church, and no one was there except him and Tonya. He had asked her for a ride to church. That didn't stop him, he taught for about two hours that day. As we were getting ready to leave, I invited him to come by the house and explained I could take him home later. He had the nerve to tell me that he would have, but that he didn't want Tonya to take the long drive back by herself. I couldn't believe him. There were only three of us there, him, Tonya and me. He was telling me that he cared more about Tonya driving by herself than he did about me driving by myself. So I got into my car and drove away. When I had let the anger bubble up inside me long enough I called him on the phone and let him have it. We didn't speak to each other for days after that.

9

Darkness & Despair

The girls decided to plan a trip to Orlando toward the end of February. I started checking different hotels for a three bedroom place. It would be Pastor Phil, Tyaja, Tonya, Machell, Kelsi, and I. Everyone would put there monies together to rent the place for the weekend. I found a place and made our reservations. The week of our trip, Pastor Phil and I got into another argument and were not speaking again. I don't even remember what we argued about but I told Tyaja that I wasn't going on the trip anymore. She was really upset and she went to talk with her dad. She called me back the next day and said that her dad didn't want to go so if I would change my mind it would just be us girls going on the trip. I agreed to go. She said they would pick me up on Friday.

Friday came and I got off work and went home to pack my bag. The girls arrived at the house in a van. I went and told my family I was leaving and went outside to put my bag in the van. As I opened the van door there was Pastor Phil. When I saw him I was shocked. The girls came over to talk to me and said that they had talked him into coming. I was still angry with him but I didn't want to upset the trip so I told them I would go but I wasn't saying anything to him. So we drove there and got to the hotel late that night. Tonya and Tyaja shared a room, Machell and Kelsi shared the other room, and Pastor Phil and I shared the third room. He stayed on one side of the bed and I stayed on the other. We didn't speak to each other at all. We got up the next morning and we all got dressed to go to Islands of Adventure. We got to the park and Tyaja needed my annual pass to get the discount on the other tickets. Pastor Phil gave her my pass and she went on to get the tickets. We got into the park and went on all the rides over and over. Tyaja came to me and told me that she still had my annual pass if I wanted it. I replied "Yes". She knew that I had been asking Pastor Phil for it for months and he refused to give it to me every time. So finally I had it.

We had lots of fun at the park then we went to Universal Studios. While we were there Pastor Phil came over to talk to me and I gave in and spoke back to him. By the time we left the park, we were back on speaking terms. We all went and got something to eat and then returned to the hotel feeling tired. As we got dressed for bed, Pastor Phil started talking to me about different topics on relationships. I could tell this conversation would not lead to anything good. All of a sudden, as we were lying in bed and I was practically falling asleep, Pastor Phil asked me if I would have a ménage a' trois. My eyes opened wide and I said "What?". He repeated the question and I said "No!". Then I thought about it and I said " With who?" Because in the back of my mind this man was asking me if he could have sex with Tonya and have me be a part of it, but he never said her name. He just simply replied "it doesn't matter." So I said to him "It does matter. I want to know if you want us to have sex with another woman or another man. I want to know if you think that I would watch you have sex with another woman or if you would watch me have sex with another man." Then I said to him "you're right it doesn't matter because I'm not doing it. Besides didn't you say that God told you to keep it Holy?" He would always say that the marriage bed is undefiled. It was like a plate with all the things that you loved to eat on it. In marriage, you could have any and everything that you wanted from that plate. Your only restriction was to keep it Holy. So I said to him "How is letting someone in our marriage bed keeping it Holy?" He stayed quiet for a long while and I started to fall back to sleep. Then he started up again about having a three-some and I kept telling him that I wasn't doing it. He began to get more and more adamant with his tone to the point that I hardly slept that night. I was so happy to see daylight and as the sun came up Pastor Phil got up and went out of the room to Tyaja's room.

I got up after he left and went to take my shower. All of a sudden he came slamming on the door asking for my annual pass to the park. I told him that I wasn't giving it to him. He started shouting at me telling me that he wanted my card and that I was going to give it to him. That started an argument as I came out of the bathroom. I told him that he had a control problem. He had no reason for wanting to hold onto my annual pass card other than to hold it over my head that when I wanted to go to the park I would have to ask him for it. It was not his card, I paid for it with my own money and there was no reason for him to keep it especially since we were not living in the same house.

Then he started telling me how much he hated me and how he didn't want to be with me. I told him that was a good thing, because I didn't want to be with him either and that no one in their right mind would want to be with him. He told me that Sister Harriet wanted to be with him and that he had slept with her while we were married. I told him that Harriet only wanted to be with him because they had never lived together. But, had they ever lived together she too would want to run away from him. Then I told him that I didn't care if he slept with Harriet because the two of them deserved each other. Then he said that he wished that he had never married me. I told him so do I, but unfortunately, I was still his wife and he could go and tell Harriet that.

Then he stretched his hand out and shoved me in the face. He pushed me so hard that I fell back. My hip bone hit the corner edge of the lower tiled step of the Jacuzzi tub and the back of my head hit the upper tiled step of the tub and I rolled to the floor. As my head hit the floor my eyes looked at the ceiling and I remembered thinking, "Am I going to die here today?" He came over to where I had landed on the floor and started kicking me in the face and in the stomach and stomping his foot on my head. I did not scream, I didn't make any noise other than the sound of my body hitting the concrete floor and steps. I don't know why, I kept quiet; I must have been in shock. I managed to get up and I started hitting him back. By this time, the girls must have heard the scuffling and they came running over. He then picked me up by my arm and slung me over his back and slammed my back to the ground and was getting ready to hit me when the girls held him down and eventually got him out of the room.

Pastor Phil went outside, while the girls came back to ask if I was alright. I told them what happened and that I was going to call the police. But, first I called my brother Sammy and told him that. Next, I called the police and they came over. When they got there Pastor Phil hadn't came back yet. I told them everything that had happened including that I had hit him back in self defense. At that point, Pastor Phil came back and he told the police that I had attacked him first. He told them that I started arguing with him about another woman named Harriet. The girls spoke to the police, but they couldn't tell the police who started the fight because they weren't there. In the end, the police took both of us to jail.

We rode in the back of the same police car to the police station and never said a word to one another, we didn't even looked at one each other. As I sat in the car riding to the jail, I thought about the fight and Pastor Phil telling me that he had slept with Sister Harriet. I realized that the vision that he had over a year ago concerning my next husband as he put it must have been him. He must have been seeing himself but did not recognize that he would be capable of doing such a thing. After that I closed my eyes and prayed. As I began to pray I heard a voice say "It is severed." I saw a curtain tear from the top to the bottom as if

> *After that I closed my eyes and prayed. As I began to pray I heard a voice say "It is severed" and I saw a curtain tear from the top to the bottom as if God Himself had ended this marriage and that was my release.*

God Himself had ended this marriage and that was my release.

When we reached the police station they separated us. I went to the female section, and he went to the male section. I was charged with domestic violence, patted down, had my picture taken, got my finger print taken, was told to remove all my jewelry, hair accessories and even my bra because it was the under-wire type. I was allowed to keep the rest of my clothes on. I was then taken to a holding cell. It was Sunday afternoon and I now had to make the call to my house to let them know where I was. It was the hardest thing for me to hear my son Kamrin answer the phone and hear the message tell him that it was a collect call from the Orlando prison. He was crying on the phone and asking me what had happened and I had to tell him that pastor Phil and I had a fight at the hotel. Then he put my sister Lyla on the phone and I told her where I was and what had happened. I told her I would call back because they couldn't call me and that I was to be arraigned the next morning. I was given a blanket and later some food on a plate that was so old that it looked like it was taken straight out of an Oliver Twist movie, with some meat, butter beans and bread.

There were about five females including myself in the holding cell. Some of them began telling their stories of why they were in there. One of them asked me what I was charged with and I told her domestic violence; she told me about her fight with her boyfriend. When I got my blanket and finally lied down and closed my eyes, it felt as if God just rushed in like a flood. When the spirit of God came to me I felt my eyes begin to blink uncontrollably and I just cried silently in my blanket. I cried and prayed until I fell asleep. Every time I woke up I felt as if God was letting me know that He was with me.

The next morning I called the house again and found out Lyla and Frances were on their way to Orlando. I asked them to make a three way call to Kara so she could pray with me. My boss Tony answered the phone and I spoke with him first. He said that he and my cousin William were working on a bondsman to get me out, then he put Kara on the phone and she prayed for me.

Right after that, I was taken before the judge to give my plea. As we walked to the court room I saw Pastor Phil. He looked so evil. It was as if I could literally see a demon in his face and that demon was saying "I'm going to get you!" It left me with a chill. I will never forget that look on his face. I was given a court appointed attorney who spoke to me and when my case number came up I pleaded not guilty and the judge told me that my spouse and I could not live in the same house and that I would have to move but I told him that we did not live together. He said that I would get a date in the mail and I was free to leave on bond. I was then taken back to the holding cell to wait to get bonded out. I waited there for hours. I started to get nervous because the guard came over to the holding cell and said that she would be coming back to take everyone to the showers and then take us to the general population which was the big prison. I did not want to have to take my clothes off and take a shower in front of them and I definitely did not want to go to the big prison.

About twenty minutes later, three names were called and the last one called was mine. I was so happy that I had been spared the experience of the shower and the general population prison. When I got out I saw Lyla and Frances and hugged them and thanked them for coming for me. They took me to the bondsman office where I signed some papers, then headed home. I was never so happy to be going home. I slept in the back seat the entire trip. I was so gracious to everyone for getting me out. I heard that Kamrin had called his dad and everyone in the islands knew what had happened. I also heard that Pastor Phil was still in jail because Tyaja had to try and raise the money for his bondsman so he didn't get out until a few days later.

After I settled in at home, for some reason, I felt very afraid. I was still feeling lost. I felt that I had lost myself and my personal power. I had become someone that I didn't even recognize. I wasn't my usual jovial self.

That person was gone. I would walk through the house in fear, thinking that I would turn around and find Pastor Phil there. I would leave work, get home, and check outside to ensure he wasn't anywhere around, and then I would run to the front door to quickly get inside. Once inside, I would check every room, every closet, and behind every shower curtain, thinking he had gotten or would get inside the house. I was traumatized and fear was crippling me. I would see his face everywhere.

A few weeks later some of the people from Pastor Phil's church started calling me, telling me that I should get back with him, that he loved me and how he was sorry for what he had done. They told me that it was partly my fault, so I shouldn't hold him completely responsible. I told them that I was not coming back to him or the church. Then they started telling me all kinds of things: how I was not going to be blessed, that I was not in the church that God had put me in, and how I was out of the will of God. One of them even told me that God told her to tell me that if I didn't come back to Pastor Phil and the church that I was going to die. I told her that everyone was going to die and so was she. Pastor Phil had tried to kill me; therefore I would go along with what I heard, which was, "It is severed."

10

Restoration

I was still just a hollow shell and still did not know the person I had become. I didn't smile, I became cautious about everyone, and was not willing to let anyone into my cocoon. I made the decision to go to Pastor Chaney's church. At the church service, I saw the pastor's wife who smiled at me and hugged me. I leaned slightly forward to hug her, but barely moved my arms. I felt physically frozen, only without the chill, and I could not smile back. My body was there, but that was it. The old happy Mable was somewhere deep, deep inside this torn down, beaten down, psychologically fragile being and the only thing they still had in common was their eyes. Through the eyes of this crushed soul, the old happy, smiling Mable could get a glimpse of people, and her surroundings but she couldn't respond to them. It was almost like looking through a thick glass wall.

When the pastor came in during praise and worship he walked up to the front. He began to speak about one topic but then started to talk about things that reflected my recent life. Then he said that his sermon was changing and it was not him. He said that he didn't know why he was discussing what he was, but it must be for someone in the church. He talked about going to jail, that real men don't hit women, that men of God don't hit women. Then he looked at me and told me that I was a blessed woman. He said that the things that have been an obstacle in my life in the past 3-6 months were being moved out of my way because God is taking me to another level. He went on to say that I was a thinker, that I thought too much and wanted everything to be perfect and in place. He reminded me "But, only God is perfect". He said God was taking me to another level, because I had power which I knew not of and my power was in my mouth, but I didn't know who I was in Christ. He said that I would never be the same. It felt as if God were taking a bulldozer and pushing all that stuff out. He said that I had been in a situation for about three years that had been nothing but an embarrassment to me, but God was getting ready to release me. He asked me if I believed that what God allowed was for my good, and if I could see the good in things that are bad. He said that the closer a lie is to the truth, the longer it will stand, but what does light have to do with darkness? God can take what was meant for bad and turn it into good.

Then he preached to the congregation, the Bible states that the last thing to be tamed is the tongue and that it was the trick of the enemy to have us talk negatively about another person. He said that we want to see everyone else negatively in order for us to see ourselves as perfect, but this is really something that one sees as a shortcoming in themselves. We have to both learn and receive the word of God. The obedience that we do is better than any sacrifice we could make. He quoted Philippians 4:6-9 "Be careful for nothing, but in everything by prayer and supplication with thanksgiving let your request be made known unto God and the peace of God which passes all understanding shall keep your hearts and minds through Christ Jesus. Think on things that are good. Whatsoever things are true, honest, just, pure, lovely, of a good report, of virtue, of any praise, think on these things. The things which we've learned, received, heard, and seen in Jesus, that's what we must do and the God of peace shall be with us."

Pastor Chaney called me out to the front of the church and he said to me "God really loves you and you are beautiful. The devil tried to take you out. He tried to drive you crazy or kill you and he used your husband to do it. Your husband was called of God to preach the gospel, but he got so intertwined with other things that he's about to lose his mind.

He's about to die spiritually and he doesn't even know it. He has said many things and he can be downright mean and tried to make you think that it was you, but in Jesus name it is not you, it is not you, it is not you."

Then Pastor Chaney asked me if my husband and I were together at the time and I replied "No". He said to not even think about going back right then, because he wasn't ready. He told me to go on a fast for three days and after three days if my husband did not repent, that God was going to sever it.

He said that my husband could be dangerous, but that God would take him out of there, because he knew just enough to be devilish and conniving. He continued by saying that my husband knew too much about God, because he is called of God, therefore he can be dangerous. He said that he was called of God, but was being led by Satan. He said that I have not even told the whole story about my situation and what was done to me and that it was church folk who had done it. Then he told me if I hear anything that was contrary to what God said, I was to put my hand over my ears and speak the words Jesus, Jesus, Jesus and this would release peace in me. He prayed that I would have peace in my mind. He also told me that I had about three or four books in me and that I would be instrumental to the finances of the church.

A few days later I spoke to Minister Lowe. He said that Pastor Phil told him that he didn't know what happened to him, that he blanked out, and he would have probably killed me if Tyaja and the girls didn't come in the room. I eventually spoke to Pastor Phil on the phone and knew that he was lying about the incident. He told me that he loved me and I told him that he never did.

In April I filed for a divorce. At first, Pastor Phil wanted to give me a hard time and not sign the papers. Then he wanted half of everything I had, but we had been married for a little less than three years. My house was purchased long before we got married so it was not common property. The only thing that was bought during the marriage was his car and I didn't want that, but I did want my name off the note so he had to refinance it in his name. Eventually he was served and given twenty days to respond, which he did not. The divorce was granted in July when we appeared before a judge. That was the last time I saw or heard from him.

Even though the marriage was over, I still had lots of healing to do. I continued attending Pastor Chaney's church, until I finally got my smile back. I also continued going to Kara's Bible study on Thursday and she would pray with me every day at work. Kara told me that God was going to restore me. She said that God wanted me to know that He had me covered, that nothing could touch me, and that nothing could come near me, because I had made God the Most High my dwelling. She told me that God wanted me to pray every day, that He would visit me, give me scriptures, and that He wanted me to write everything down. So I did, and He did. Every day as I prayed, the Lord would give me scriptures to read. Here are some of the ones I heard and wrote down:

The first day I heard "Be still and know that I am God". Then I heard Ezekiel 3:4 "A watchman over the house of Israel. Go and speak to them. Tell them what thus saith the Lord. If you don't then their sins are required to your hand. If you do and they don't listen, then it's not on your hand. If you do and they listen, then you've won a soul."

The second day I heard "Be still and know that I am God."
Then I heard Romans 3:4-17 "God forbid: yea, let God be true, but every man a liar that thou might be justified in thy sayings, and might overcome when thou art judged: and John 3:16 "For God so loved the world, that he gave His only begotten Son, that whosoever believes in Him should not perish, but have everlasting life".

The third day I heard Romans 3:5 "But if our unrighteousness commend the righteousness of God, what shall we say? Is God unrighteous who taketh vengeance? I speak as a man".

Then, **Romans 5:17** "For if by one man's offence death reigned by one, much more they which received abundance of grace and of the gift of righteousness shall reign in life by one, Jesus Christ".

The fourth day I heard Psalm 91

"He that dwelleth in the secret place of the most High shall abide under the shadow of the almighty. I will say of the Lord, He is my refuge and my fortress, my God, in Him will I trust. Surely He shall deliver thee from the snare of the fowler and from the noisome pestilence".

On the fifth day I heard Galatians 4

"Now I say, that the heir, as long as he is a child, differeth nothing from a servant, though he be the lord of all; But is under tutors and governors until the time appointed of the father. Even so we, when we were children, were in bondage under the elements of the world; But when the fullness of the time was come, God sent forth His Son, made of woman, made under the law, to redeem them that were under the law, that we might receive the adoption of sons. And because we are sons, God hath sent forth the Spirit of His Son into your hearts, crying Abba, Father. Wherefore thou art no more a servant, but a son; and if a son, then an heir of God through Christ"

Then I heard Psalm 23.

At first I wasn't going to read it, I was just going to say it. Then God told me to read it and the words came alive. I realized it was a love letter to me.

The Lord is my shepherd - He is my protector, he looks after me.

I shall not want - He provides for me everything that I need, I shall have no lack and no desire that is not met and taken care of by Him.

He makes me to lie down in green pastures - He has blessed me with a good place to lay my head. He has given me a beautiful place to rest. It is green pastures meaning it is full of life and growing still.

He leads me beside the still waters - He is taking (leading) me to a place of peace and tranquility. There are no calamities in my life that He can't handle. I don't have any rough seas because he's already given me the assurance that he's with me and he will bring me through. Lo, I am with you always even until the end of time. He wants me to have His peace which surpasses all understanding.

He restores my soul - when I am down He picks me back up. He dusts me off and restores me back to Him. He keeps me in fellowship with Him.

He leads me in the path of righteousness for His name sake - He keeps me on the right path so that I will bring his name glory. He teaches me to keep his word so that I will glorify His name and make Him proud of me.

Yea though I walk through the valley of the shadow of death - even when I go through things that may frighten me or I may go through dark times and face obstacles that may seem to overpower me, I realize that it has not come to take me out for it is only the shadow of it.

I will fear no evil for thou art with me - I do not have to be afraid because God is with me.

Thy rod and thy staff they comfort me - Jesus professes his love for me. In the dictionary of my Bible I looked up rod and staff. The rod, which was 3 feet tall was used to fight off wolves and other animals that were dangerous to a shepherds flock. The rod was used to prod or push their flock over rough country and was made typically of hardwood sapling and ending with a bulging knob. The staff was about 5 feet tall and was used to lean on and rest while watching their flock. Also used as a source of direction for the Shepard to direct the flock into an enclosure, into a place where we could be protected. Here God is saying that His rod and His staff are there to comfort me. He will protect me and keep me from all harm. When the enemy comes in like a flood (Isa 59:19-21), He is there. And His Spirit shall raise up a standard against him. And the Redeemer(Jesus) shall come to Zion for those of us who have turned from sin. God say this is His covenant with us "His spirit that is in us and His words that He has put in our mouth, shall not depart out of our mouths, or from our children's mouths, or from our children's children's mouths. So if we just let him, He will lead us and guide us into all truths.

Thou prepares a table before me in the presence of my enemies- You can't do anything, but fall to your knees when God has made your enemies your footstool. When he has made your face strong against their faces and your forehead strong against their forehead as Ezekiel 3 says. He will allow the enemy to see you being blessed even amongst a barren land. When everything seems like it should be going bad for you, your head is still held high amongst your peers. They look at you and wonder how you've made it through. Oh, but God. If we notice, when God vindicates you, when God gives you victory, when God brings you through, He does it in the presence of your enemies. Why? Because he wants to make sure that the word gets out about "your" GOD. He wants a reputation of being your God, your deliverer, your strong tower to precede you. He wants your enemies to fear you, His child, even before you get there. Because He's been your provider all along, He's fought your battles all along, He's kept your head above water all along. He's been your back bone all along, He's been your tear dryer all along, and He's been your burden bearer all along. That's how you made it through.

Thou anoints my head with oil, my cup runs over - After He's cleaned me up and restored me back to Himself, He fills me with His anointing. He covers me, he blesses me with more than I can ever even think of because it is His good pleasure to give me the keys of the kingdom. I am His chosen vessel whom He has entrusted with all power in heaven and in earth and in whom He is well pleased. That which I loose on earth is loosed in heaven and that which I bound on earth is bound in heaven.

And after all this, **Surely His goodness and His mercy shall follow me all the days of my life and I Shall dwell in the house of the Lord forever.**

The sixth day I heard Genesis 1.

And once again, I was not going to read it because I knew that it was about when God created the earth. And once again He urged me to read it. So I read it, and it talked about the firmaments, and how God divided the day from the night, and dry land from the waters and calling the dry land earth and the water He called the seas. It talked about how God put the stars in the sky, and how God made man and all living creatures. And I didn't understand how that related to me and my situation. I prayed and I said God tell me what this means to me, and I got no answer. Then as I got up from praying and walked towards the bathroom, He said Mable and I said yes, and God said "if I can create the earth and everything in it, don't you think I can take care of you?". I fell to my knees and cried "Yes Lord, you can, I get it now Lord, now I understand".

The seventh day was Mark 5 which had three wonderful stories that I felt had everything to do with me.

The first was of the demoniac man with the unclean spirits and how Jesus called it out of the man and when people saw the man again he was in his right mind. This reminded me of the familiar spirits that I had seen torment Pastor Phil and how those spirits were transferred to torment me and send me into my downward spiral but through the power of Jesus Christ it was called out of me and He was now bringing me into my right mind, restoring me back to me through the reading of His word. This scripture also spoke about the woman with the issue of blood who touched Jesus' garment and was made whole. How just by having faith in the power of Jesus you can be made whole from your plague. I was now being made whole from my plague by the increasing of my faith in Jesus. The third was of the damsel that had died Jesus tells the people not to weep she is not dead, she is only sleeping. He then takes the girls hand and says "Talitha cumi" which means Damsel I say unto thee, arise. This for me was Jesus picking me up from my ashes, from my dead and dark spot and telling me to rise up, wake up and get on with the business of living, be about the business of fulfilling your destiny. And Mark 15 which talks about the crucifixion of Jesus when He cries out Eloi, Eloi, lana sabachthani (My God, My God, why hast thou forsaken me?) and after His death the veil of the temple was torn in two from the top to the bottom. I had this same feeling that God had left me, that God hated me but at the moment of my darkest hour God rushed in and made me realize that He was always there. It was I who walked away from Him and stopped communicating with Him. Seeing a curtain tear from the top to the bottom was also my experience when God released me from my torment and said "it is severed".

The eighth day I heard Isaiah 44 "Yet now hear, O Jacob my servant, and Israel whom I have chosen: thus saith the Lord that made thee, and formed thee from the womb, which will help thee; Fear not O Jacob, my servant and thou Jesurun, whom I have chosen. For I will pour water upon him that is thirsty, and floods upon the dry ground; I will pour my spirit upon thy seed, and my blessing upon thine offspring.….)"

Then I heard Mark 11 which talks about Jesus riding into Jerusalem on the donkey. It also talks about Him cursing the fig tree and it withering away. Then it says if we have faith as small as a mustard seed, then we shall say mount be removed and it shall be moved. But we have to have no doubt in our heart and we have to believe that the things that we ask for shall come to pass, then we shall have it. We also need to forgive others or God will not forgive us our trespasses.

Next, I heard Psalm 27

"The Lord is my light whom shall I fear. He is the strength of my life, whom shall I be afraid. When the wicked, even my enemies come against me, they stumble and fall. One thing have I desired of the Lord, that I may dwell in the house of the Lord all the days of my life and to behold the beauty of the Lord and enquire in his temple. In the time of trouble He shall hide me in the secret place of His tabernacle shall he hide me".

And Psalm 81

"Sing unto God, make a joyful noise unto the God of Jacob; For He removes your shoulder from burden, and your hands from the pots. When you call in times of trouble, he delivered you. He answered thee in the secret place of thunder"

And finally, I heard Romans 8

"There is therefore now no condemnation to them which are in Christ Jesus, who walk not after the flesh, but after the Spirit. For the law of the Spirit of life in Christ Jesus hath made me free from the law of sin and death. For what the law could not do, in that it was weak through the flesh, God sending His own Son in the likeness of sinful flesh, and for sin, condemned sin in the flesh; That the righteousness of the law might be fulfilled in us, who walk not after the flesh, but after the Spirit. For they that are after the flesh do mind the things of the flesh; but they that are after the Spirit, do mind the things of the Spirit. For to be carnally minded is death; but to be spiritually minded is life and peace".

11

Final Words

After the experience in my marriage to a pastor and being a member of his church, I would say to you to guard your spirit, and guard your mind. Be careful what you allow to take root in your soul. Make sure that it is of God.

Originally when I saw Pastor Phil preaching and talking with God and God talking back with him (or what I thought was God), I wanted that. I wanted that close relationship with God, where I could hear from God and talk to Him and He could talk to me. In my innocence, I became fascinated with his gift, and his anointing. In my ignorance, my fascination of prophecy and my decision to continue visiting the Bible study, was the bait that Satan used to lure me into his plan. The gift of prophecy was enticing and a gift that God truly gave to him without repentance as the Bible states. This means that even though Pastor Phil had perverted himself, God wasn't going to take it away from him. I did not discern what was in operation, and I coveted this ungodly ability he had to tap into the unseen realm through familiar spirits and divination. It wasn't the true gift of God that I coveted, as 1 Corinthians 12:31 tells us to, **"But covet earnestly the best gifts".** It was simply his demonic ability to know hidden things. God knew the dangers of coveting long before we were created, which is why He included it as one the ten commandments.

Most of us don't realize what it means to covet but Webster's dictionary says to covet is to wish for earnestly, to desire what belongs to another without regard for the rights of others, to desire wrongfully. [4]Concerning coveting, we need to acknowledge that **1)** it doesn't belong to us, **2)** we can't handle what comes along with it, and **3)** we need to stay in our own lane and allow the Holy Spirit to activate our own spiritual gifts.

Desiring hidden knowledge leaves an open door for familiar spirits and spirits of divination. These unholy spirits can be transferred from one person to another through many different ways. It can be transferred through the laying on of hands, through words, communication, or associations with bad people, through sexual activity, through watching TV and films, through books, music, food, jewelry, soaps, perfumes, ritual idols and many other objects. [5]

My acceptance of the slippers from Pastor Phil was a transference of his divination spirit that led to my false visions. The first vision that I had on the cruise of my friend Cindy having twins was a false vision as it did not come to pass. I also learned that slippers, shoes, or footwear represent your walk with God. This would explain my separation from God through Pastor Phil's manipulation. The demonic force that was already in him saw that weakness in me, and latched on to me with its intent to destroy me and my desire for God. My visions of marriage to Pastor Phil came as a part of that divination to entice me into an unholy soul tie. After the marriage, I never had another vision, at least not like those.

Those visions played more like watching an old slide show movie. The ones where you had to place the filmed frame in front of the light of movie camera and have it display on the big screen. Those visions went from one screen shot to another. They also usually happened right after a dizzy spell or light headedness. Now if I see a vision it's like a still life picture, a one frame picture, and it happens while I am praying. For example, I was praying with lady and when I closed my eyes in prayer I saw her standing in an old white nurse's uniform with a matching nurse's hat. After prayer I told her what I saw and she told me that she was in school to become a nurse but she never finished and she wanted to get back into nursing school.

Once in the marriage, and the vow was made before God, only God could break it, except for the sake of adultery, at which point I would be free to leave the marriage. All along, I thought God had a plan for ministry for us, but in fact it was the enemy's plan to get rid of me. God's word says in Jeremiah 29:11 "I know the thoughts I think toward you, thoughts of peace and not of evil, to give you an expected end." My marriage was not peaceful but full of evil. It was my own curiosity to learn about the God I saw in him. That's what I was looking for and that's exactly what I found, but it was not the One True God. Once the enemy had done its job of crushing and shutting me down and separating me from God, then he was ready to discard of me. This is what Satan does with you after he's destroyed your life and this is why Pastor Phil was ready to discard of me by putting his plan into action to discredit me and tear me down. This is also why he could move so easily from person to person. Destroying each life as he goes on, and using religion to carry it out. All he has to do is just find the next God hungry person and there's usually quite a few of them in church.

I later learned that what Pastor Phil was operating in is called a "Python" spirit of divination. It is very subtle and very common in the church. Like the snake, it seeks to suffocate and choke the word and plan of God in the lives of its victims. Its victim can be the church, an individual, a family, or an entire community. Through the use of deceptive, unauthorized prophesies it seeks to dominate and ultimately kill its target. Once under its power, one experiences a sense of spiritual detachment and disinterest that leads to the stifling and strangling of your natural and spiritual interests and desires. This then leads to feelings of desperation, disheartenment, and desolation and then ultimately to wanting death [1]. The python spirit also works in unison with a beguiling, and seducing Jezebel spirit which uses lust, greed, and pride to turn people away from God [2]. One of the characteristics of this is a spirit of control. Those in spiritual leadership can more easily use the Bible to control or place fear into the hearts of people, and they do it all in the name of the Lord. They use the Bible to manipulate their own agenda. Another characteristic is guilt and condemnation. You are made to feel that you're going straight to hell because you don't follow their views or beliefs and by disagreeing with them you are disagreeing and disobeying God. Yet another clue, is that they do not like to be questioned on their beliefs or viewpoint. Once you are caught up in that spirit or being blinded or controlled by someone with the python spirit, you begin to eat it up. You begin to see them as your god. You don't even hear God anymore for hearing them. You begin to feel frightened, frail, and fatigued. This leads us to another characteristic which is that they exalt themselves and become driven by titles (3). Pastor Phil literally called himself God and used scripture to back it up. Deception can come through the spoken and written word of the bible through misuse and the ill-intentions of the user.

Ask yourself this question, "Are they of God?" I am not referring to their position, be it a preacher, prophet, evangelist, etc but their lifestyle. Examine the words that they speak. Are they producing good fruit? Divinations and familiar spirits are often so subtle that it may be difficult to determine under which a person may be operating under, whether it be of God or of Satan. Note that there will always be some truth being said mixed in subtly with each lie. We must remember that one percent untruth makes the whole thing deceptive and false.

In the Bible, Paul says to follow him as he follows Christ.
It implies that if I am not following Christ, if my negative actions start to become a familiar pattern for me, if I continuously choose to do that which is wrong and out of character for Jesus, then do not follow me.

Healing Prayer for Defilement of Divination

If you identify with anything that I have shared or if some part has touched you in some way I would like to offer a prayer that you can use as guide for your spiritual healing.

" Heavenly Father, I humbly come before you and open up to you. I repent and pray your forgiveness of all my sins. I pray that you clean me up Father, for I know that where I am weak you are strong. I pray your forgiveness for the spirit of covetousness. For you said in your commandment that we should not covet our neighbor's goods. I pray Father that you forgive me for having my eye on the sensationalism of prophecy and the chasing of your word by false means rather than relying and learning of the one true God who can discern all things. For you are truth and light, wisdom and knowledge. I denounce all ungodly soul ties, and I break the bondage of all its affects on my life, in Jesus name. I denounce Satan and all his evil works, in Jesus name. I curse and bind every demonic trick of the enemy intended to seduce me into idolatry and divinations, in Jesus name. In Jesus name, I uproot every familiar spirit and spirit of darkness and command it to flee from me for it has no authority over me. By the authority of Christ, I cast down every vain imagination that seeks to exalt itself above the authority, knowledge, and plan of God for my life; and bring my every thought into submission to the obedience of Christ; for I am a child of God, and heir of the King. My heart's desire is to please God and to be found worthy in His sight. I pray God that you create in me a clean heart and renew within me a right spirit and a right relationship with you. I thank you God that by having an intimate relationship with you, I have access to everything I need for you are the author and finisher of my faith.

In your Son, Jesus' name I pray. Amen."

Sources

(1) Discerning Divination by Michele Perry http://www-fromtheunpavedroad.com/2010/09/09/discerning-divination/

(2) Spirit of Python by Bobbie Jean Merck http://www.carpenterstouch.org/gpage8.html

(3) Divination by Jimmy Lathan http://truthcontinuum.tripod.com/Divination.html

(4) Webster Dictionary

(5) Transference of Spirits by Friday Okoh http://www.faithwriters.com/article-details.php?id=37745

(6) https://en.wikipedia.org/wiki/Divination

www.ingramcontent.com/pod-product-compliance
Lightning Source LLC
Chambersburg PA
CBHW050602300426
44112CB00013B/2033